Learning to Teach

Jonathan Glazzard, Neil Denby and Jayne Price

Open University Press

Open University Press
McGraw-Hill Education
McGraw-Hill House
Shoppenhangers Road
Maidenhead
Berkshire
England
SL6 2QL

email: enquiries@openup.co.uk
world wide web: www.openup.co.uk

and Two Penn Plaza, New York, NY 10121-2289, USA

First published 2014

A catalogue record of this book is available from the British Library

ISBN-13: 978-0-335-26328-8
ISBN-10: 0-335-26328-3
eISBN: 978-0-33526329-5

Library of Congress Cataloging-in-Publication Data
CIP data applied for

Typeset by Aptara Inc., India

Praise for this book

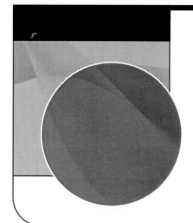

Contents

CHAPTER

1

Introduction

Links to Teachers' Standards

This is a general chapter so all groups of the Teachers' Standards will apply with equal importance.

Introduction

Welcome to the world of teacher training! That you have decided to learn about the art of teaching is a great credit to you. It is not, as some might believe, a natural skill bestowed on those who have good knowledge of their subject, but one which must

be learned, practised and honed. Training to teach is what your mentors, tutors and host teachers will tell you that you are doing; **learning to teach** is what you will actually be doing. There is a world of difference between 'training' and 'learning'. 'Training' evokes ideas of drill, repetition and rote learning; these are not what teacher training is about.

Having good subject knowledge may be a necessary condition for good teaching, but it is not a sufficient one. Think of all the great teachers of ancient history – on the whole they were generalists, not subject specialists. Aristotle taught a range of subjects and skills, and taught them in a non-didactic (or instructional) way. His pupils were involved and engaged in active learning long before the term was coined.

What Aristotle did was to encourage learners to question, to debate, to explore the limits of their abilities. Skills, knowledge, even attitudes are only of use to the learner if they are learned in such a way as to be transferable. This means they need to be not just learned, but also understood.

Preparation

While you may well start out observing others, helping a small group (maybe high flyers, maybe those that are struggling) or team teaching, you will, sooner or later, be left on your own with a class to teach. In many of the new routes into teacher training, this may be almost immediate and the expectation might be that you start teaching from Day 1. You therefore need to be prepared. Part of that preparation will have been built in as part of a good interview process for your course, so you will have been into schools, planned lessons and studied the curriculum of your chosen subject and age range.

You should also have begun to find out where your knowledge is strong, and where it might be lacking. To do this, you will need to look at a current text for your subject at the level that you will be teaching. This will show you both the breadth and depth of subject knowledge needed. Your own degree level knowledge is likely to be fairly narrow and esoteric. You will have specialised – for example, as an English graduate in particular writers or sets of literature, or in developing styles of writing and argument; as a scientist, you will have specialised in a major branch – perhaps even a branch within a branch, astrophysics perhaps, or marine biology; as a historian in a particular period or angle of history. Unless your degree subject was 'education' (and for many of you, it will have been), then you are, almost inevitably, a specialist. This means that a great deal of the syllabus at GCSE or A level may be unfamiliar to you – in particular, the level at which it is taught – so it is something that you need to brush up on.

Rationale

It is not without some apprehension that we choose the writings of Sun Tzu to provide a framework. He is inextricably linked with the waging of war. But he was, first and foremost, a great strategist, as well as a successful general, and his principles have been adopted in numerous successful business books. In no way are we suggesting that the classroom is a battleground – what we are suggesting is that it is what a strategist would call a 'situation'. A situation is one in which there are variables that are within your control, and some that are not. The approach taken below recognises this situation is one in which there are three main players – yourself, the pupils and the system in which both work together. The system ranges from the micro – dealing with pupils on a one-to-one basis according to school rules, to the macro – the school itself, its masters (LEA, governors or academy/free school sponsor) and, ultimately, the government and its education policy.

Sun Tzu

Sun Tzu provides advice on recognising what is positive and what is negative about your situation and how to maximise the positives and minimise or eliminate the negatives.

- **Opening moves.** Your opening gambit has to be that you are going to establish your own presence and your own boundaries in a class. This is your space and you have to own it. This may be difficult to begin with, and you may have to do some hard yards before your authority kicks in – but it is essential. So, to begin with, you must be clear who you are, what you want the pupils to see you as, and how you are going to achieve this.
- **Planning.** Lessons and schemes of work – and your routes through them – need to be carefully planned. This can be done in the tight confines of a school template or other provided lesson plan, or in the more organic methodology provided by mindmaps or spidergrams. Either way, you must know not only what you are doing, but when, why and how. You must also be clear on what you expect learning outcomes to be, and how you will assess progress towards them.
- **Waging war.** Recognising the 'opposition' and neutralising them before they can attack is a key part of strategy. First, of course, pupils are not the 'enemy' (although you will frequently hear teachers referring to them as such – with affection). Second, it is your knowledge of them and interest in them that will bring them 'on side'. This is a fine balance – you are not a teenager, so professing interest in the latest boy/girl band or fashion fad is more likely to alienate you than include you, while, for example, a working knowledge of computer games or a shared interest in sport might provide common ground.
- **Strategies.** This refers to the 'how' of your teaching. What are your strategies for teaching and learning; for maintaining good behaviour; what are your back-ups in case of breakdowns (e.g. in technology)?; your alternatives if x or y doesn't work, if the internet goes down?; if the pupils have been detained

elsewhere so are late to your lesson …? Over and above all of this, what are your strategies for delivering learning?

- **Dispositions.** This could include where you teach and how you position yourself – and the support of persons or artefacts in the classroom. Your teaching space itself is one of the variables that you need to order into the shape and style that you want. You can have it set out as a classroom – desks in rows and separate – but is this what you really want? Is it better sometimes to have 'cabaret' style set-ups so that group work is easier; is a 'herring bone' pattern better for facilitation; sometimes a circular layout may be best. Maybe you don't need the desks at all – or, in some cases, chairs, because of particular activities that you intend to try. This all adds interest and variety to your teaching delivery. Think also about the way that you position yourself in the room. For instance, don't always teach from that 'position of power' behind the teacher's desk at the front of the room. Learn to move about and place yourself at the best position for what you want to achieve and for what you want the pupils to achieve.
- **Forces.** One of the central planks here is going to be your subject knowledge – from reading current texts and examination specifications, rather than specialised degree knowledge. Such knowledge and expertise are of no use to you, however, unless you can express them with clarity and enthusiasm. So what can you bring to the table? A variety of approach, coupled with activities, a sense of humour, your own interest and enthusiasm and empathy with student issues of understanding. Essentially, it is how you engage pupils in their own – pupil-centred – learning.
- **Strengths and weaknesses.** Take stock of what you have going for you and what you have going against you, both in terms of yourself and the school situation in which you find yourself. Be honest, and look to build on your strengths and minimise your weaknesses. Strengths could include confidence, determination, fairness, consistency, certainty and respect. Weaknesses could, effectively, be the opposite of these: not following through, using sarcasm and insult, condescension, lack of confidence, lack of preparation or knowledge.

Sun Tzu sees the ultimate victory as knowing enough about your enemy not to have to go to war. Ultimately, your preparations, tactics and strategies are such that battle does not have to be engaged. This is what good teaching is all about.

Standards

Currently, you qualify as a teacher by providing evidence that you have reached certain pre-set standards. These 'Standards for the award of Qualified Teacher Status' are laid down by the Department for Education (DfE) and the Secretary of State. Although some commentators will tell you that you don't need such standards, that you can teach without them as long as you have good subject knowledge, this has been proven time and time again not to be the case. Good teaching needs to be learned, it is not a skill that tends to come naturally. Having excellent subject knowledge within, for example, a degree does not mean that you can impart understanding to pupils. Similarly, having an excellent technical background does not mean that you can teach skills effectively.

There are two parts to the Teachers' Standards: teaching and personal and professional conduct (duties and responsibilities). The teaching part of the standards is divided into eight groups as follows:

1. *Set high expectations which inspire, motivate and challenge pupils.* This set covers the teaching environment and the way that the teacher should model the positive behaviours she or he wishes to promote. It also contains the single most important standard – that teachers should set goals that stretch and challenge pupils of all backgrounds, abilities and dispositions. This therefore covers differentiation, planning lessons, assessment and feedback and the central skill of knowing where pupils are in terms of attainment, and how to move them on to improve.

2. *Promote good progress and outcomes by pupils.* This group also includes having prior knowledge of attainment and building on this. Teachers should also know the theory of how children learn and be able to apply this appropriately to teaching. Pupils should be encouraged to take some responsibility for their own work and progress.

3. *Demonstrate good subject and curriculum knowledge.* A group of standards that emphasises the importance of appropriate subject knowledge, with specific reference to synthetic phonics for English teachers and appropriate strategies for the teaching of mathematics.

4. *Plan and teach well-structured lessons.* You are expected to have a knowledge and understanding of effective curriculum design and to adapt this to ensure effective use of lesson time. This includes the role of homework and of improving through reflection on your own learning.

5. *Adapt teaching to respond to the strengths and needs of all pupils.* You should develop differentiated approaches to cater for all abilities and needs that you teach. This includes knowing what factors might encourage or inhibit learning and building on or minimising these as appropriate.

6. *Make accurate and productive use of assessment.* To know where pupils are in terms of current attainment and progress requires you to assess work and to provide useful and developmental formative and summative feedback. You should also know how to use the various data that exist to support assessment and progress.

7. *Manage behaviour effectively to ensure a good and safe learning environment.* Behaviour should not be a problem as long as pupils are motivated and engaged with their learning. You should learn to set expectations for behaviour and to provide a framework of rules to encourage good behaviour. You should demonstrate fairness, good management of classes, the use of praise and reward and sanction systems.

8. *Fulfil wider professional responsibilities.* This set of standards may well be the most important in securing you a job in a competitive market. They refer to your contribution to the wider life and ethos of the school and your own professional development. The former may be the key difference between you and another candidate – you have run the chess club, the debating society, extra music lessons to help progress, supported school teams, coached the football team ... whatever it is, it has added to your role and importance in the life of the school. These standards are about your relationships with other staff and your professionalism, but are also an indicator of your enthusiasm and commitment. In terms of professional development, they refer to your ability to be reflective and self-critical, but also how well you take and apply advice from others.

Pedagogy

Pedagogy is a term that you will hear often on your course, but maybe never again afterwards! It is derived from the Greek and effectively means 'to lead the child'. It refers to the set of tactics, techniques and strategies that you use to ensure that learning takes place. Note, it does not mean 'to push' the child, or 'to cram the child with knowledge'. It is not about drill, or exposition, it is about leading the child to the learning via enquiry, interest and motivation – a very Aristotelian view of teaching and learning. If you were a magician, it is what spells you have to turn your teaching into learning.

Conclusion

Whichever of the myriad routes into teaching that you have chosen, you will eventually become a competent, probably good, possibly even excellent, class teacher. You will be amazed at your own fortitude and dedication. You will learn first to cope with, then to understand, and finally to shape the complex interactions of classrooms and their occupants.

You will start out with varying degrees of support – you may have the chance, for example, to observe other teachers at work; you may have the opportunity to discuss progress and techniques with experienced members of staff; you may have preparation and marking time that is protected from the predations of the timetable. These are likely to be increasingly rare opportunities once you develop a busy full-time teaching role, so you must take full advantage of them while you can. Take the opportunity to learn from others, monitor and reflect on your own progress and to develop your own professional techniques and solutions. In teaching, there is no problem in copying what others do if it is effective; you don't have to create your own techniques and strategies from scratch, but you can learn from observation, and adopt and adapt as necessary to your own situation. Learning why a particular method or way of working is good for someone else, and then developing it as part of your own style, is a central part of the process of learning to teach.

What we have learned

- Subject knowledge is important, but not everything
- Preparation is the key to good teaching
- Good knowledge of pupil attainment is essential
- A teacher needs to be an all-rounder, contributing to all aspects of school life
- We can learn by observing others
- Self-criticism and self-reflection are major factors if we want to improve

Advice and ideas

Reflection is a skill that is natural to all of us, so don't think of it as a barrier to your progress. When coming out of the cinema, or after a meal, or any shared experience, a person's natural inclination is to ask the others 'did you enjoy that?', 'what did you think of it?', 'what were the best/worst features for you?' Classroom experience is one that you share with pupils, mentors and other observers, so don't be afraid to ask these questions of them (yes, the pupils too) and of yourself.

What do you think . . .

...are the pupils expectations of you, as a teacher? Think about when you were a pupil of the same age as those that you will be teaching. How did you expect your teachers to treat you? What sort of a relationship did you think you would have with them? Did you expect your education to be teacher-led and teacher-centred, or for it to be a collaborative venture? Finding out from your new charges how they expect to be taught (some of which may be shaped by former teachers) will help you to build how you want to teach them.

Problem

There are some teacher duties that you will inevitably have to perform. One of these is the legal obligation to take an attendance register. Sometimes, this is just first thing in the morning, sometimes morning and afternoon, sometimes, especially where there are issues of internal truancy, at the start of every lesson. This can turn into a negative and annoying chore. Less successful strategies that you may witness and which tend to diminish its importance include:

- Having someone else (perhaps a teaching assistant) do it

- Having the pupils do it for themselves
- Looking around the room and taking an almost surreptitious register so as to avoid engaging with pupils
- Barking out a list of names. (You end up with your pupils' names etched on your brain: Archer, Aston, Barker, Brent, Brown, Carter, Carter, Denby …).

How do you think you can stop this from happening and make it a positive part of a lesson?

Solution

Think of how many ways there are of taking the register – you should make it part of your cycle of observations. Successful strategies that can make it an addition to the learning time of the day include:

- Insistence on total silence and attention while reading out a list of names. This can be used to create a pool of calm and a clear indicator that the lesson has started. It develops good habits.
- Creation of such a pool of calm – and then using it to engage with pupils to show your knowledge of them, and concern for their welfare. This could be subject- or lesson-specific comments: 'I enjoyed the piece you wrote for homework'; 'impressive bit of research, there'; 'do you think you are now clear on what we meant?', or at a more personal level: 'hear the team did well on Saturday'; 'hope you're feeling a bit better now'; 'early days, I know, but how are you coping with Ramadan?'.

If positive relationship building can be derived from register taking, then it is worth doing even when it does not have to be done due to the existence of, for example, swipe systems.

Recommended reading

Buitink, J. (2008) What and how do student teachers learn during school-based teacher education? *Teaching and Teacher Education*, 25 (1): 118–27.

Day, C., Kington, A., Stobart, G. and Sammons, P. (2006) The personal and professional lives of teachers: stable and unstable identities, *British Educational Research Journal*, 32 (4): 601–16.

Department for Education (DfE) (2013) *The Teachers' Standards*. Available at: https://www.gov.uk/government/uploads/system/uploads/attachment_data/file/208682/Teachers__Standards_2013.pdf.

2 Observations

Links to Teachers' Standards

Standards Part One: Teaching
Standards Group 4: Plan and teach well-structured lessons
Standards Group 5: Adapt teaching to respond to the strengths and needs of all pupils

Introduction

There are three stages to your observations in schools. Before even securing an interview, you first need to have some recent experience of a school of the age range in which you want to teach. You may have been out of school for some time (big changes

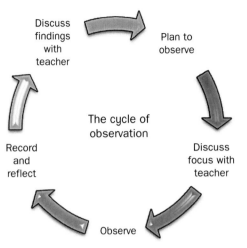

Discuss findings with teacher

Plan to observe

The cycle of observation

Record and reflect

Discuss focus with teacher

Observe

can happen in just a few years) and your school experience is likely to be limited to your own (often fondly remembered) alma mater.

Second, once embarked on your course, one of the best ways to learn effective teaching and learning skills is to see others apply such skills competently and professionally. Such observation must be clearly structured. It may be focused on the teacher, or on a particular interaction between teacher and pupil or teacher and a group of pupils.

The third stage is the formal and informal observations of your teaching. Throughout your training and later career, you will be observed – by mentors, tutors, department heads, head teachers, even Ofsted inspectors (and, in the fullness of time, by those trainees that you are mentoring yourself). These observations are a key means by which your progress is measured and assessed.

Before you start

Observations are an integral part of interview processes for most teacher training courses. As part of your preparation you should observe in at least two schools. The reasons for this are so that you know what to expect – this is why observing in two schools is better than one – and so that you can judge for yourself whether this is really 'for you'. The last thing that any institution that accepts you at interview wants is for you to start a placement in September with the realisation that 'this is not what you expected'. Don't visit your old school. It is unlikely to provide any insights or surprises (apart from the realisation that nothing really does take place in the staffroom). Ensure that you have properly prepared for the observation. Read the curriculum for the subject and, if appropriate to the age range and, examination specifications. Know if the subject (and school) sit inside or outside the National Curriculum. Have an awareness of how national strategies and priorities might impact on teaching and learning. Be clear on Key Stages and age ranges so that you avoid gaffes (there is no Key Stage 5, for example).

You will be observing but the class teacher who, in many cases, will provide a report to your interviewers, will also be observing you. This neatly exemplifies the two sorts of observation that will occur throughout your school career – observations **by** you and observations **of** you.

Observations by you

Prepare for the observation by talking to the teacher, planning a focus and deciding on your role in the lesson. Key questions for you should be who to watch, what to watch and what can you learn from this.

The 'who' are other classroom practitioners of different subjects and different levels of experience. We use the term 'classroom practitioners' deliberately here, as you may not always be watching teachers, but may focus on other practitioners, such as teaching assistants, technicians or specialist colleagues supporting second language learners or other discrete groups.

These observations will help you to understand the impact of teaching on how children learn and will introduce you to techniques that you can adopt and adapt in your own teaching. Such observations must always be with the express permission of those you are observing. Observations are much more powerful if you discuss them with those you have observed. You are not in a position to be critical of practice or practitioners, so should confine your discussions to what you have seen (or think you have seen) and questions as to why events and interactions have taken place. It is also possible that the interactions that you are observing are not caused by what you think they are caused by. There are many variables that you may not be able to see. For example, try to watch the same lesson delivered to two different classes, or the same group in consecutive weeks and compare teaching and learning. What changed the 'mood' of the classroom? It may be something obvious (like a football team winning/losing) or something much more subtle. If you can note such changes, you can then make the positive ones work in your favour and minimise the effects of the negative ones.

The ones to watch

Watch experienced teachers [formerly these may have been assessed and designated as Advanced Skills Teachers (ASTs) or Excellent Teachers (ETs)]. These are teachers who have shown that they possess excellent classroom skills. Ask your mentor who are the staff to watch – he or she will know, by rumour and reputation, which teachers teach lessons that inspire and motivate pupils, because they will have heard pupils talking about them. Different teachers will demonstrate different skills and strengths. Some will have command of humour; some will have an encyclopaedic knowledge of their pupils' backgrounds and interests; some will have an infective enthusiasm for their own subject.

Watch those who have specific skills, experience or qualifications and see how they operate. Examples include those who are supporting children with physical or learning difficulties; who are helping children who do not speak English as their first language; or children who are particularly bright or gifted. In the primary classroom observe how one-to-one or small group teaching works. Whether primary or secondary, you should make sure that you also observe lessons that are not directly linked to your own subject specialism or area of expertise. A PE trainee, for example, may learn much from watching a physics lesson, and vice versa. You could even watch fellow trainees' lessons and see if you can gain any insights (and provide supportive feedback and criticism), thus combining being observer with being observed.

How to watch

A disciplined observer is clear on what he or she wants to find out, even if it is phrased in general terms such as 'Was that lesson a success? And if so, what made it so?' Before

Name	John
Photo: Gender = M	
Ethnicity	WB
Language spoken at home	English
FSM?	No
Physical	Should wear glasses: reluctant
SEN	G+T
Other	Likes cycling, fidgety, don't sit with Abel

Name	Marie
Photo: Gender = F	
Ethnicity	WEE
Language spoken at home	Czech
FSM?	Yes
Physical	Slight hearing, sit on left
SEN	EAL
Other	Still at silent stage, needs lots of support

long, however, you will need to decide on a specific focus for your observations. Sometimes you will be looking at **what** has happened – so it may be a question of frequency, or regularity, or even severity. Sometimes you will be looking at **why** something happened, taking a sharper focus. You will therefore be collecting both quantitative data (how often, how many, how long) and qualitative data (why did that happen?; what caused that interaction?). Typically, there will be a combination of the two – so you might count how evenly the teacher treats boys and girls (how many times she or he speaks to each gender) and then formulate theories on how this affected the course of the lesson.

At the outset decide, with the class teacher, whether this is to be a passive or an active observation. You can be a 'fly on the wall' or 'outside observer' – or you can be just another person in the lesson. If you decide to be active, perhaps through facilitating or working with small groups, the pupils are unlikely to react. Unlike in the past, they are now used to many additional adults working alongside them in the room. The data you collect is important, so you must be thorough about how it is recorded. Quantitative data can be easily recorded on tick sheets, interactions less easily so, but a seating plan of the classroom and a data pack (such as shown) will help.

What to watch

Watch what might be called the 'dynamics' of the lesson. These are the interactions between the teacher and pupils, pupils and other pupils, teaching and learning, activities and interest, activities and demonstrated learning. You may want to divide this into two – management of the classroom and management of learning.

Management of the classroom includes: how pupils enter and exit the room; how they are greeted at the door; how the teacher makes the space his or her 'own'. You should observe how the space is used – is it flexible?, is the use of it effective?, is this the best use of it? Management of resources may also come under this heading. Remember resources include everything supporting the lesson, including equipment, books, lesson materials, interactive whiteboards, technology and support staff. In terms of effectiveness, how is lack of engagement or misbehaviour dealt with? How does the teacher ensure that pupils remain on task? Some of these may be looked at in terms of frequency (e.g. the number of times quiet has to be called for; the number of rewards or warnings issued) or in terms of quality (e.g. the relative effectiveness of individual praise and whole-class praise). Consider how effectively the lesson has been planned and is 'chunked', and how well changes in activity and emphasis help to maintain engagement.

Management of the learning includes: the objectives of the lesson and how these are communicated to pupils; how the lesson starts, the number and variety of activities; the way that transitions between activities are managed; the use of different groupings; the use of questions and explanations; the use of assessment to support learning; the place and purpose of the plenary. Again, sometimes these are quantitative (e.g. number of questions asked), sometimes qualitative (e.g. the way in which questions are targeted or differentiated). Differentiation refers to the way that different learning outcomes are expected from pupils of differing ability, meaning different teaching approaches, materials or support are needed. You should also observe the pace of the lesson – in particular, changes in pace and how these are appropriate to improve learning. Observation may also be pupil focused. You should look at a particular pupil or group of pupils in different situations – perhaps tracking a pupil through an entire day, or watching how a pupil reacts and interacts with teachers when different teaching and learning methods are employed. This could be focused further – for example, you could observe how a pupil with English as an additional language (EAL) or emotional or behavioural difficulties (EBD) is supported throughout the day.

Observations of you

The first time you will both observe and be observed is at the pre-interview stage. In the classroom, expect your experience to develop into more than just observation. You may, for example, be asked to show that you 'have it in you' to be a good teacher by facilitating, helping small groups in a class, or by team teaching. Key questions about your suitability to teach include how flexible and adaptable you are and whether you can respond to changes and new situations in the classroom. Can you provide lucid and appropriately age-related explanations? Are you secure in your subject knowledge? Do you appear to have a personality that relates well to children?; that uses humour appropriately?; that displays confident body language? Are you patient and supportive? As part of the selection and interview process, you are likely to have to provide evidence of this time you have spent observing teaching and learning – and answer questions linked to it. You will not be surprised to learn that an observation of you teaching is a key part of the job interview process.

Observations as an assessment tool

While you may well start out observing others, helping a small group or team teaching, you will eventually be left on your own. You will be observed many times during your teaching practice. Observations are an assessment tool, used to gauge your progress, to highlight strengths as well as weaknesses.

Observations, which will be used as a tool of assessment throughout your career, are the principal tool for assessment and an aid to professional development. According to Lasagabaster and Sierra (2011: 449), 'researchers and practitioners generally agree that the most effective use of classroom observation is for professional development'. These observations will both look at your general progress, and at how well you are reaching specific standards. Agree a focus with your mentor to help you progress. You could decide to look at generic issues like behaviour or pace, or at specifics like starters and explanations of difficult concepts, or your use of support staff.

Once you are a qualified teacher, there is a limit to the number of observations that can take place during an academic year (usually understood as three plus any Ofsted observations, but subject to local agreements). As a trainee, there is no limit. This is good, as you should welcome as many supportive comments and criticisms from fellow practitioners as you can gather.

Primary and EYFS

Lesson observations will focus not just on teaching but also the quality of your learning environment and how well it impacts on the progress of the learners. Working walls help children to make progress by providing 'tools for learning'. A mathematics working wall can be changed on a weekly basis according to the focus of the unit of work. Include worked examples, key mathematical vocabulary and examples of the everyday application of mathematics using photographs of shapes, patterns or word problems. A literacy working wall should include a good example of the text type you are teaching and examples of the vocabulary and punctuation choices that you want pupils to use to enrich their writing. You can provide additional tools to support pupils' learning within lessons, including number squares, number lines, alphabet mats and spelling mats or dictionaries. The observer will focus on how well your pupils are using the tools to accelerate their progress in the lesson, rather than displays serving no other purpose than as wallpaper.

Observing your pupils

You will use observation as one of your own tools to determine whether the pupils you are teaching are making progress. In the early years you will make many of your judgements about pupils' learning by observing them and noting what they know and can do. You can collect evidence in the form of written observations of children, photographs or digital evidence (but see Chapter 3 on safeguarding). For EYFS, observations can be subsequently analysed and linked back to the Development Matters statements. This will help you to plan the children's next steps in learning.

Formal and informal observations

Observations may be formal or informal. On occasion, you will be informally observed in the same way as other members of staff if your lesson is on a 'learning walk' or chosen for a 'drop-in'. Learning walks are planned by senior members of staff and involve them calling in on lessons for brief periods. Sometimes you will receive informal feedback from a mentor or host teacher who is working with you in a classroom, or who sees a particular part of your lesson. Formal observations are less frequent, and will link your performance and progress directly to the teacher standards. You should therefore take them as an opportunity to find out your strengths and what you still need to work on.

Observers will expect a lesson plan, a data pack on pupils and a copy of any resources being used. They will need to know where the lesson fits in a series or scheme of work and the criteria for judging whether pupils have made progress. If it is a mentor observation, agree the focus beforehand. An external observer is less likely to do this, but you might ask a tutor to focus on a specific element where you feel you have developed or improved. Sometimes you will be observed by more than one person (a joint observation), with them having the intention of comparing notes to ensure consistency.

Just as important as planning and the actual lesson is the feedback. Evaluate your lesson honestly yourself – what went right, what went wrong, what worked and what didn't. Then listen to the feedback. You should expect feedback that is constructive rather than destructive. Be receptive, not defensive. Remember that observers have an unbiased eye, a better view than you and a wealth of experience.

Conclusion

Observations – by you of teachers, by you of pupils, and of you – are a central part of learning to teach and improving your teaching. They should be welcomed as supportive and helpful. You may have the undoubted benefit, on some teaching routes, of your initial teaching efforts being 'off-the-job'. Teaching a lesson to fellow trainees in a 'safe' setting is an excellent way to try out techniques and receive feedback. If this is not possible, you might want to think about using technology to observe yourself. Arrange to have a lesson videotaped (this is a facility already available in universities and many training schools) and then observe it with a critical eye. All the positives that you are looking for in your observations are the areas you should be demonstrating. All the negatives are the areas you should be avoiding.

What we have learned

- Observations by you or of you are a key feature of training starting before interview
- Observations need to be planned and focused
- A key part of observation is discussion and feedback
- Observations are used for your professional development

Advice and ideas (1)

You can be a 'fly on the wall', or you can be just another person that is helping out in the lesson. One analogy is driving a car. If you wanted to observe how well someone was driving, you could do it from inside or outside the car. When watching a Grand Prix race, for instance, you would judge from the outside. With a new driver – for example, a learner driver – you would judge from inside the car. One is a 'fly on the wall', the other is as a passenger – a participant-observer taking part in the journey. In either case, you would need to develop a set of criteria by which you are making the judgement. Some of this is going to be quantitative – how fast, how many gear changes. Some of it is going to be qualitative – how smooth is the ride, how good are the gear changes. Try to apply the same logic to your lesson observations. Not only what you are looking for, but why it is important.

Advice and ideas (2)

Observations may even count towards the 'time in school' required for teacher training. Some courses let you 'carry' the days, so this is worth checking.

What do you think . . .

... it feels like to be a pupil? One of your early observations should be to follow a single child's school day. This will let you see the highs and lows of the day, where teaching has been effective (and why) but, more importantly, will help you to empathise with pupils and understand, perhaps, why they become tetchy, uncooperative and tired.

Problem

In one multicultural primary classroom, pupils worked in different sized groups (individuals, pairs, threes and fours, whole class) with the changes between each group being marked by the whole class counting down from ten to one in a language nominated by one of their number. So for one transition it was 'ashra, tiss'a, thamania, sab'a' (Arabic), for another 'shi, jeou, bah, chi' (Mandarin), and so on as each pupil suggested their own language. What are the important features of this? What should the observer be looking at?

Solution

Quantitative observation could be on the number of transitions or the number of languages used. Qualitative observations, on the other hand, could reveal a richness to the approach that had adapted a 'control' mechanism to show that each pupil's native language was valued, while also teaching other pupils a little of it.

Recommended reading

Department for Education (DfE) (2012) *Pupil Behaviour in Schools in England,* Research Report DFE-RR218. Available at: https://www.gov.uk/government/uploads/system/uploads/attachment_data/file/184078/DFE-RR218.pdf.

Galton, M., Hargreaves, L., Comber, C., Wall, D. and Pell, A. (1999) *Inside the Primary Classroom: 20 Years On.* London: Routledge.

Lasagabaster, D. and Sierra, J.M. (2011) Classroom observation: desirable conditions established by teachers, *European Journal of Teacher Education,* 34 (4): 449–63.

Montgomery, D. (2002) *Helping Teachers Develop through Classroom Observation.* London: David Fulton.

3

Your responsibilities – child protection and safeguarding

What this chapter covers

- The importance of knowing school safeguarding policy
- Different types of abuse and how to recognise them
- Dealing with suspected abuse or a disclosure
- Responsibilities related to bullying
- Responsibilities related to e-safety

Links to Teachers' Standards

Standards Part Two: Personal and Professional Conduct
Teachers must have regard for the need to safeguard pupils' well-being, in accordance with statutory provisions. These refer to your duties and responsibilities in regard to personal and professional conduct.

Introduction

A number of high-profile cases in the media in recent years have highlighted the devastating effects of child abuse. More recent cases in the media have drawn attention to breaches of professional trust by teachers who have been accused of abusing their pupils. This chapter examines categories of abuse and provides practical guidance for trainee teachers and beginning teachers in the event of a disclosure of abuse or suspected abuse. Safeguarding pupils' wellbeing is a responsibility that all schools and teachers must take seriously. Schools should be safe places for pupils because if pupils are not safe or if they do not feel safe, they are unlikely to learn effectively.

Under the Education Act 2002, all schools have a legal duty to safeguard and promote the welfare of their pupils. Schools are legally obliged to create a safe learning environment and in cases where there are concerns about a child's welfare, schools must work in partnership with other organisations to take action to address these concerns.

The safeguarding policy

All schools have a statutory duty to provide a safeguarding policy and all staff working in a school need to know and understand their duties in relation to this policy. Safeguarding training should be part of the induction process when a new member of staff joins the school. The school's designated safeguarding officer will need to attend biannual face-to-face training and all other members of staff will need to complete this training once every three years. Many schools and teacher training institutions now purchase online training packages for individuals to complete in addition to the statutory training which they are required to attend. Schools are required to appoint a designated safeguarding governor who is responsible for monitoring compliance with legislation, school and local authority policies on a regular basis. Any safeguarding concerns should be discussed with the nominated governor. The school policy should explain how the school's recruitment processes comply with safeguarding legislation. In addition, it will explain specific procedures that need to be adopted in relation to suspected abuse or disclosures of abuse. It should also explain how allegations of abuse against staff members will be addressed, as well as providing an overview on policies related to restraint, handling, contact, photographing pupils, collecting other digital imagery and whistleblowing. You need to be aware of these policies and of the types of abuse that exist.

Types of abuse

There are four broad categories of abuse:

- **Physical abuse** includes throwing, shaking and hitting a child or subjecting a child to other forms of physical harm. It is also considered physical abuse if parents, carers or other adults deliberately induce illness in a child.
- **Emotional abuse** refers to the persistent emotional maltreatment of a child. Examples of this include:
  - making fun of what they say
  - telling a child that they are worthless, unloved or not valued
  - making fun of what children say or how they communicate
  - ignoring them

- overprotecting them
- preventing children from participating in normal social interaction
- bullying, including cyber bullying
- causing children to feel in danger or frightening them.
- **Sexual abuse** involves enticing or forcing a child to take part in sexual activities. It may or may not involve violence and the child may or may not give their consent. Furthermore, the child may or may not be aware what is happening. Examples of sexual abuse include:
  - involving children in looking at or producing sexual images
  - encouraging children to watch sexual acts
  - grooming a child in preparation for abuse, including using the Internet
  - penetrative acts, including rape or oral sex
  - non-penetrative acts, including touching, rubbing, kissing or masturbation
  - encouraging children to behave in sexually inappropriate ways.
- **Neglect** is the persistent failure to respond to a child's psychological or physical needs. This can have a detrimental impact on a child's health. Examples of neglect include:
  - substance abuse during pregnancy
  - lack of food, clothing or shelter
  - abandonment
  - failure to protect a child from physical or emotional harm
  - lack of appropriate supervision
  - lack of access to appropriate medical care
  - lack of attention to a child's basic emotional needs.

Signs of abuse

Signs of sexual abuse (Glazzard, 2012) include:

- changes in a child's behaviour
- rejection of physical contact
- evidence of bruising and marks in the genital area and/or other areas of the body
- drawings which demonstrate advanced sexual knowledge
- overtly 'forward' relationships with other children
- rocking
- being withdrawn
- stained underwear
- pain when going to the toilet
- use of inappropriate language.

Children suffering from abuse could appear withdrawn and they may appear to get easily upset. They may lack confidence, crave attention or become aggressive. It is important to point out that while any warning signs do not mean that abuse is taking place, you have a duty to report any concerns to the designated safeguarding officer in school.

Pupils with special educational needs

Pupils with special educational needs are vulnerable to abuse. Some of these pupils may have difficulties in communicating this abuse. All staff should remain vigilant and be alert to possible signs of abuse.

Dealing with suspected abuse

If you suspect abuse, you must follow the procedures that are clearly documented in your school's safeguarding policy. You should produce a written record of your concerns and include the date and time of the record. You have a duty of care to share any concerns with the designated safeguarding officer.

Physical contact with pupils

The school safeguarding policy should outline policies on touch. There may be occasions when it is necessary for you to use some physical contact, such as when a distressed pupil needs comforting. In these situations you should use your discretion but if the policy states that no contact should be made, you should adhere to this. Repeated touching (such as putting a hand on a pupil's shoulder) may lead to questions being raised. You are advised to limit physical contact with pupils and to touch pupils only when absolutely necessary. Staff must never make gratuitous physical contact with pupils.

In certain situations it may be necessary to restrain pupils. These include incidents where pupils are:

- committing a criminal offence
- causing personal injury or damage to property
- causing injury to themselves or others
- prejudicing the maintenance of good order and discipline.

Minimum and reasonable force should be considered when:

- the potential consequences of not using force are sufficiently serious to justify the use of force
- the chances of achieving the desired result by other means are low
- the risks associated with not using force outweigh the risks associated with using force.

Whistleblowing

All staff who work with pupils have a duty of care to protect them from harm. If the conduct of another member of staff gives you cause for concern, you need to follow the school whistleblowing policy. This will be outlined in the school safeguarding policy.

Photographs and other data

The school safeguarding policy will have clear guidelines in relation to taking photographs of pupils. You must never take photographs of pupils using your own camera or other electronic devices. Always use equipment purchased by the school for this purpose. Furthermore, you should not transport photographs of pupils (or other sensitive information) away from the school. If data is stored on a school laptop and the laptop is taken home, it must be password protected so that information does not end up in the wrong hands. Parents and carers must provide their consent for photographs of their child to be taken. This is vital if the image is to be uploaded into a public arena such as on the school website.

There are some general principles that you should adhere to:

- Never upload photographs of children or young people onto a social networking site.
- Do not display images of children and young people that are likely to cause upset or embarrassment.
- Avoid naming pupils or only use first names.
- Photographs should depict pupils in appropriate ways; for example, pupils should not be wearing revealing clothing or clothing that may cause embarrassment.
- Children should not be photographed for the press without parental permission.

There may be occasions when photographic or other digital evidence may need to be collected to support assessment judgements. Schools should have clear policies in place for what happens to this evidence after the assessment judgements have been confirmed.

Security of school premises and pupils

Head teachers and governors have a duty to ensure that the school premises are secure and that children will not be exposed to harm. External doors should be locked so that the building is secure and all visitors should report to the main office to sign in and collect an identification badge. Schools should take steps to ensure that all adults who enter schools are safe to be in close proximity to children. Schools will expect adults to be in receipt of satisfactory clearance returns from the Disclosure and Barring Service. However, there are exceptions to this rule, especially in cases where adults will not be left in sole charge of pupils.

Bullying

Bullying has four key characteristics. It is:

- repetitive and persistent
- intentionally harmful
- designed to create an imbalance of power
- designed to cause feelings of distress, fear, loneliness and lack of confidence.

The Equality Act 2010 protects people from direct and indirect discrimination on the grounds of disability, gender reassignment, pregnancy and maternity, race, religion or belief, age, sex and sexual orientation. The schools' White Paper *The Importance of Teaching* (DfE, 2010) stated the government's determination to reduce bullying and expressed concerns about the level of homophobic bullying in schools.

Bullying can fall into specific categories, as follows:

Verbal	Name calling
	Teasing
	Threats
	Rumours
	Ostracism
	Gossip
	Alienating
	Inciting hatred
	Taunting
Non-verbal	Intimidating gestures
	Stealing or hiding someone's property
	Dirty looks
	Written threats
	Stalking
	Shunning
Physical	Beating
	Biting
	Choking
	Kicking
	Punching
	Shaking
	Slapping
	Tripping
	Spitting
	Hitting
	Poking
	Throwing
	Shoving

	Urinating
	Groping
	Ignoring
	Blocking the way
	Being forced to do unwanted things in front of others
	Having belongings stolen or destroyed
	Sexual abuse
	Threatening with a weapon
	Using a weapon to inflict harm
	Physical assault
	Happy slapping
	Criminal damage
Technological	Threatening or intimidating e-mails or text messages
	Internet forums
	Instant messaging
	Internet chat rooms
	Social networking sites
	Creating web pages to intimidate, psychologically damage or threaten an individual or group
	Sharing humiliating video clips or pictures
Homophobic	Use of derogatory language such as homophobic comments
	Verbal
	Non-verbal
	Physical
	Technological
Disabled	Verbal
	Non-verbal
	Physical
	Technological

Schools should take all incidents of bullying seriously, and all schools should have a clear policy that details procedures for tackling bullying. Schools should take a proactive approach rather than simply reacting to situations when they arise. This should be part of the school's personal, social and health education curriculum. The taught curriculum should aim to foster respect and tolerance towards everyone, including those from minority groups. This should be reinforced through the hidden curriculum. These are the subconscious messages that pupils internalise from being in school. As well as being explicitly taught to pupils, positive attitudes can be fostered through pupils being exposed to images, texts and other resources that celebrate diversity. When bullying does occur, schools should adopt a zero tolerance approach and this should be articulated in the school's policy. Incidents should be dealt with and recorded and follow-up actions should also be logged for future reference.

E-safety

All schools should take a proactive approach in educating pupils about how to keep safe online and about the dangers of cyber bullying. Pupils need to be taught about the dangers associated with viewing inappropriate material and how to access support if they become a victim of e-bullying. Many schools have now developed their own progressive e-safety curriculum and initial teacher training providers now embed this aspect into their courses.

Conclusion

Schools need to take all the necessary steps to ensure that children are safe. The school's safeguarding policy and practices will be rigorously scrutinised during Ofsted inspections to ensure that the school is a safe place for pupils to learn. Schools need to be able to demonstrate to inspectors that they have taken all reasonable steps to protect pupils from harm. If inspectors judge that the school is inadequate in relation to safeguarding, the overall effectiveness of the school will be deemed to be inadequate. It is impossible to totally eradicate risks from pupils' lives but schools and teachers need to do all that they can to keep children safe from harm. Adequate training during your initial training and continued professional development will ensure that you feel able to meet your obligations in relation to safeguarding.

What we have learned

- You understand your responsibilities in relation to safeguarding
- You are aware of the different categories of abuse
- You know how to deal with a disclosure of abuse or suspected abuse
- You know about the different types of bullying

Advice and ideas (1)

Pupils can make a disclosure of abuse at any point during your professional career, including during your initial teacher training. Consequently, it is important that you understand the processes that you must follow should this occur. You must ensure that you are familiar with the school's safeguarding policy because this will explain clearly the steps you need to take. The following is some general advice (Glazzard, 2012):

- stay calm;
- offer reassurance to the child;
- tell the child that you are pleased they are speaking to you;
- do not offer assurances of confidentiality but explain to the child that in order to help them you will need to tell other people;
- tell the child who you will pass the information on to;
- listen to the child and let them talk;
- remember that children tend rarely to tell lies about abuse but they may have tried to tell others about it and not been believed;
- tell the child that it is not their fault;
- check that you have understood correctly what the child is trying to tell you by repeating the information back to the child;
- praise the child for speaking to you;
- reassure the child that they have a right to be safe and protected;
- do not tell the child that what they have experienced is dirty, naughty or bad;
- do not offer any comments about the alleged offender – your role is to listen to what the child has to say and to remain neutral;
- at the end of the conversation thank the child for speaking to you and remind them who you are going to pass the information on to and why this is necessary;
- remember that children may retract what they have said, so it is important to keep a written record of the disclosure;
- following the disclosure, make a detailed record of the conversation using the child's own words only; ensure that you do not add your own interpretation or personal opinion;
- never speak to a child's parents or carers about the disclosure;
- following the disclosure, it is important to pass the information onto the head teacher and/or the designated person.

Advice and ideas (2)

If you need to speak to a pupil 'in private', it is good practice to ask another member of staff to be present. If you need to speak to a pupil confidentially, then make sure that the meeting can take place in an area where you are visible to other colleagues. It is good practice to speak to pupils in shared areas or to leave classroom and office doors open. Make other adults in school aware that the meeting is taking place. You must never arrange meetings with pupils away from the school premises. It is important for staff in school, including trainees, to be aware that private meetings with pupils may give rise to concern. Clear guidelines will be given in the school's safeguarding policy.

What do you think . . .

... is meant by 'reasonable force'? What are the issues associated with the term 'reasonable force'? As a trainee teacher you must never use force. Only staff employed in schools are permitted to use force. Once you are in post you must receive training by the local authority or by a private provider on how to use force. This will ensure that you are handling pupils in the correct way so as not to result in harm. The member of staff who has applied the force must produce a written record of the incident detailing the triggers for the decision to use force, the type of force applied and the follow-up actions that were taken. Clear guidelines should be given in the school's safeguarding policy.

Problem

A parent explains to you that their child has been a victim of physical assault and that they have instructed their child to retaliate.

Solution

Arrange a meeting with the parent and use this as an opportunity to explain the school bullying policy. Explain that the school will not tolerate any form of bullying, even if this has been done in retaliation and that if their child retaliates then they, too, will face consequences. Explain that the policy does not condone meeting violence with violence. The victim in this instance can expect to be supported by the policy and the perpetrator will face consequences if there is evidence of bullying. Explain that addressing violence with violence will only escalate the situation.

Recommended reading

Byron, T. (2008) *Safer Children in a Digital World: A Summary for Children and Young People*. Nottingham: DCSF.

Department for Education (2010) *The Importance of Teaching*. London: DfE. Available at: http://www.education.gov.uk/schools/toolsandinitiatives/schoolswhitepaper/b0068570/the-importance-of-teaching.

Glazzard, J. (2012) Child protection issues, in N. Denby (ed.) *Training to Teach*. London: Sage.

Lindon, J. (2008) *Safeguarding Children and Young People*. London: Hodder.

CHAPTER 4

Managing behaviour

What this chapter covers

- The importance of relationships in managing pupils' behaviour

- The links between motivation, engagement, active learning and positive learning behaviour

- Developing effective communication skills

- Being assertive

- Strategies for developing a positive climate for learning

Links to Teachers' Standards

Standards Part One: Teaching
Standards Group 7: Manage behaviour effectively to ensure a good and safe learning environment

Introduction

Classrooms are social spaces and therefore teachers have a responsibility to act decisively to ensure a safe and secure environment where all pupils can make progress and achieve. Behaviour management can be scary for beginning teachers because they are new to their particular learning environment and have to make relationships with large numbers of new people. Most of us are also humble enough to question how we might get thirty people to follow our instructions for the first time! It is worth remembering that the majority of pupils are keen to learn or at least to behave.

Current policy is characterised by a belief that positive learning behaviour can be taught and nurtured and that pupils' behaviour in the classroom comes as a result of a number of influences, all of which can be mediated by the teacher. Powell and Tod (2004) devised a conceptual framework outlining the influences that contribute to learning behaviour as follows:

- **Relationship with self.** How pupils see themselves as learners. If pupils feel that they are unable to succeed, it can chip away at their self-confidence as learners and they become less likely to commit and engage in working and making progress.
- **Relationship with others.** This is how pupils react socially and academically with others in the classroom. Behaviour can be influenced significantly by pupils' interactions with others, including teachers, peers and other adults in the classroom.
- **Relationship with the curriculum.** Purposeful, interesting, pupil-centred, active lessons that are focused on meaningful progress are much more likely to encourage and nurture positive learning behaviour from pupils.

It is therefore incumbent on teachers to provide learning experiences for pupils where they experience success, work collaboratively with others and which engage them while making progress in order to foster positive behaviour in the classroom.

Motivation

Pupils' motivation to learn is a major factor in their engagement and positive behaviour in the classroom (see Chapter 9). Motivation affects their interest in the topic, their persistence and resilience as they work through the tasks and the effort they put in to achieving the best possible outcome. Pupils' motivation can be influenced by intrinsic rewards such as feeling a sense of achievement, or extrinsic rewards such as teacher praise. Teachers can increase pupils' motivation by explaining the purpose of the activities they are doing and by providing opportunities for pupils to have choice in the way they are completed so that they develop a sense of ownership.

Providing stimulating resources as pupils need them, responding to their questions when they are stuck and encouraging them when they are trying hard go a long way to alleviating their anxieties when the work is challenging for them. Setting the right level of challenge is important and this relies on a really clear understanding of where the pupils are and what they need to do to progress further. Pupils may need some support at first before they can complete the work independently and this might come from teacher intervention and modelling, from supportive resources such as writing frames or from working collaboratively with other pupils.

Developing a personalised approach to learning and teaching, where individual pupils are valued and activities are planned to specifically address their needs will result in pupils who are too engaged in what they are doing to start to display negative behaviours. Personalised approaches rely on competent formative assessment for learning (see Chapter 10) where targets and feedback are individualised to the pupil.

Effective communication

The way you interact with pupils can build rapport and forge a positive climate for learning, which, in turn, facilitates learning behaviour. If pupils are greeted by an enthusiastic and committed teacher who they know enjoys working with them, they are much more likely to display positive behaviour. Enthusiasm is communicated through facial expression, tone of voice, positive language, praise, the way you greet them at the door, the way you explain key concepts and ideas and your commitment to preparing interesting, engaging activities and resources for them.

A fundamental skill you will need to develop is the ability to gain the attention of the class; it is very important that you do not talk or start explaining a concept if some members of the class are not listening. Inexperienced teachers do this because they are worried about the pace of the lesson being slow as they wait for the pupils to settle down. At the start of the lesson, an instruction to listen and a stance that shows that you are ready to start usually work. With some classes, a settling activity that the pupils work on as soon as they arrive in the classroom provides an opportunity to start the lesson formally while everyone is quiet. Aim to start the lesson on a positive note; if you are waiting for a few seconds for everyone to settle, the use of 'proximity praise' can be a useful tactic. Try saying, 'Thank you, Josh, you're ready to start', when Josh is very near to another pupil who is not quite ready. When the whole class are quiet, acknowledge it positively and move on.

Use of voice

As a teacher, your voice should be your most treasured possession. Looking after it involves learning how to project to the back of the room without shouting by careful breath control and clear enunciation, drinking plenty of water, resting it whenever you can and avoiding speaking over lots of noise. Using your voice effectively in the classroom requires you to vary the way you speak in terms of volume, speed and intonation. A really good way to become more conscious of the way you use your voice is to record a few minutes of talking in the classroom. You might be surprised by the way you sound in a recording and it is useful to analyse it carefully. Do you vary the intonation in your voice to convey emotion, urgency, a sense of importance or is it more mono-tonal? Is your speech clear? Is your accent difficult to understand? How would you describe the volume? Do you sound friendly, approachable or annoyed and in a bad mood? Do you have any distracting habits such as using 'erm' frequently or adding the word 'okay' after every sentence? One thing you should practise is consciously lowering your voice slightly when you are giving an authoritative instruction. When you get anxious, the pitch of your voice tends to get higher and this makes you sound less in control.

Non-verbal communication also needs consideration. Pace in a lesson can be maintained by using non-verbal signals rather than stopping to give an instruction. For example, signals for 'come in' and 'sit here' are useful when a pupil arrives late to the lesson, a shake of the head can say 'no, stop doing that' to a pupil, or a meaningful look can be useful to gain attention or show disapproval. Be careful not to give mixed messages to pupils though. For example, if you are trying to reprimand pupils and your facial expression gives a different message, you are unlikely to get the desired effect. Similarly, 'joking' with a class when you are trying to settle them is also confusing. Just standing in a different place can have a powerful effect on the behaviour of the pupils you are near to; you can often stop low-level disruption just by letting pupils know you have seen them and expect them to stop.

Using positive rather than negative reinforcement is an effective way of maintaining a positive atmosphere in the classroom. Tell the pupils what you want them to do, rather than telling them not to do what they are doing. For example, 'Sarah, I need you to face the front, thank you' is better than 'Stop turning round, Sarah'.

Being assertive

Learning to be more assertive can really improve the impact of your behaviour interventions with pupils. Teachers may subconsciously ask a question when giving an instruction; for example, 'Hasif, can you stop doing that please?' Practise a script that is more assertive:

- Use 'I' statements such as 'I need you to', then state clearly the behaviour you want.
- If the pupil argues, use a partial agreement statement and then restate your instruction; for example, 'Okay, I understand that, but now I need you to . . .'.
- Rather than using 'please', which signals that there is an option not to comply, use 'thank you' as a pre-emptive close to signal that you expect the pupil to do what you want.
- If the pupil continues, repeat the instruction.
- If the pupil still continues, finally giving them a choice is usually effective in achieving the desired outcome. For example, 'Hasif, I've explained that you need to get on with your work; if you continue you will get a detention, you decide.'
- Avoid reaction to 'secondary behaviours' such as slamming a book down or throwing a pen on a desk; these are attention seeking, and are usually just a last stand.
- Remain calm and speak in a normal tone; remember you are not angry, you are expecting the pupil to comply.

Being assertive is also signalled by your non-verbal communication: make eye contact with the pupil, maintain a relaxed stance, get closer, but avoid invasion of body space. Assertiveness is more convincing when you are feeling confident, and confidence comes from good planning, including differentiated materials and 'back-up' plans in case the technology does not work, or pupils complete a task more quickly than expected. Confidence also comes from using the school behaviour policy consistently. Maintaining consistent approaches to behaviour management reinforces expectations and allows staff to support each other. Understanding the school policies and strategies is a key priority during your induction period in a new school.

School policies

According to Hook and Vass (2000), the relationship between teachers and pupils is underpinned by what has become known as the '4Rs'. First, there are Rights and Responsibilities. Teachers have the right to teach, to feel safe in their classroom and to be listened to; pupils have similar rights to learn, to be safe and to be heard. The teacher's responsibilities might be defined as enabling all pupils to learn, to provide purposeful engaging activities that enable pupils to make progress, to develop a positive classroom environment; pupils' responsibilities might be to work cooperatively, to allow others to learn, to try hard. Rights are translated into Rules that are maintained by the Routines that underpin and reinforce them. Whether pupils maintain rules and responsibilities is a matter of choice. Choosing to maintain them leads to positive consequences (rewards), whereas choosing not to leads to negative consequences. The consequences of either decision are inevitable, leading to a consistent approach across the school.

Developing a positive climate for learning

Some simple approaches that can be used on a daily basis to underpin your interactions with pupils will help you to develop a positive climate for learning in your classroom, the most important of which is immediate, specific and appropriate praise. We may have a tendency to ignore good behaviour because it is what is expected, but if you reward it, you are much more likely to experience more of it. The strategy is to reward straight away, and to reinforce the behaviour you are pleased with, for example, 'Well done for getting the equipment out safely.' Some schools use stickers, stamps or team points as more tangible rewards. Appropriate praise depends on the child – sometimes you need to maintain a pupil's 'street cred' by doing it quietly, sometimes a phone call or a postcard home is appropriate.

The second approach is to be consistent. Pupils should know what to expect when they arrive at your room. Be consistent in your expectations of their behaviour and your routines, but most of all in your attitude to pupils. You may be having a bad day, but pupils will be rightly aggrieved if you are impatient with them for no apparent reason.

The third approach is to use the concept of choice. This is outlined above but is worth reiterating here. Always ensure that the pupils make the final decision to comply or not and reward them when they make the right decision. You can reinforce the notion of choice positively as well: 'Sam, I'm really pleased you've decided to work hard today.'

The fourth approach is to know your pupils' names – every strategy advocated in this chapter works better when a name is attached. You have to learn names proactively, use seating plans and memory strategies, particularly if you have a large number of pupils to teach.

The strategies for managing low-level disruption are advocated in the National Strategies Behaviour and Attendance Toolkit (DfES, 2004). These are useful tools for beginning teachers.

Strategy	Description	Example
Indirect reminder	Remind the whole class rather than individual pupils what needs to happen	'There are still resources to put away and it's nearly time for lunch'
Behavioural direction	A direct statement of the behaviour expected	'Tyler, sit still, thank you'
Rule reinforcement	Remind pupils of a classroom expectation	'Emma, what's your rule about ...?'
Diversion	Divert pupils' attention away from the unwanted behaviour	'Alright, Ben? Good, get on with your work then' 'Parveen, can you give these books out for me, please?'
Refocus	Reinforce the positive behaviour you want	'Justin, what should you be doing now?'
What, when, how	Replace 'why' questions with 'what', 'when' or 'how' questions	'What should you be doing now?' 'How will you remember to?'

Finally, teachers *and* pupils really value the notion of 'respect'. Some teachers think that they are entitled to respect because they are in a position of power and authority in the school. Pupils are much more likely to be respectful when they are welcomed into a positive learning environment, and one of the ways to do this is to show respect to pupils. Avoid 'rude' non-verbal communication such as pointing at pupils, rolling eyes and tutting. Avoid using your size to dominate an interaction such as invading body space, standing over a pupil or using aggressive behaviour. Try to listen to what pupils have to say; accept the possibility that sometimes teachers can misjudge a situation. Above all, to maintain self-esteem, if you do have to chastise a pupil, criticise the behaviour and not the child personally.

Conclusion

Pupils are much less likely to be disruptive when the teaching is engaging, when the learning activities demand active participation, when they have the right levels of support and challenge, and when they feel they are making tangible progress. Beginning teachers can learn simple strategies for managing low-level disruption, while maintaining a positive climate for learning, consistency, fairness and approachability are the keys to most things. Don't listen to anyone who tells you not to smile until Christmas!

What we have learned

- There are a number of influences on learning behaviour in the classroom, all of which can be mediated by the teacher
- Purposeful, active, engaging activities are key in maintaining positive behaviour in the classroom
- The importance of effective communication with pupils
- Strategies for developing a positive climate for learning

Advice and ideas (1)

Think carefully about how you will stop the pupils during an activity. For example, giving pupils advance warning that you are going to stop them in two minutes. If the activity is a relatively noisy one, a non-verbal cue such as one arm in the air can be useful, or an alarm on the whiteboard works well. Sometimes you might need to do a countdown from 5 to 1 to settle the pupils, giving them time to finish what they are doing (if you overuse this tactic though, you'll find it loses its impact). It is important to have something worthwhile to say if you stop the class during an activity; meaningless whole-class interventions which do not impact on pupils' progress will soon become a catalyst for pupils taking a long time to settle both to listen to you and to get back to work afterwards.

Advice and ideas (2)

Inspired by the 'Checklist Manifesto' of Atul Gawande, Charlie Taylor (2011), who was then the Government's Expert Adviser for behaviour in schools, developed 'behaviour checklists' designed for head teachers and teachers to use to help them improve behaviour in schools. He suggested that each school should adapt and personalise the lists but they should be used as a daily reminder to ensure that the correct preparations are in place.

Behaviour checklist for teachers

Classroom	
Know the names and roles of any adults in class	
Meet and greet pupils when they come into the classroom	
Display rules in the class – and ensure that the pupils and staff know what they are	
Display the tariff of sanctions in class	
Have a system in place to follow through with all sanctions	
Display the tariff of rewards in class	
Have a system in place to follow through with all rewards	
Have a visual timetable on the wall	
Follow the school behaviour policy	
Pupils	
Know the names of children	
Have a plan for children who are likely to misbehave	
Ensure other adults in the class know the plan	
Understand pupils' special needs	
Teaching	
Ensure that all resources are prepared in advance	
Praise the behaviour you want to see more of	
Praise children doing the right thing more than criticising those who are doing the wrong thing	
Differentiate	
Stay calm	
Have clear routines for transitions and for stopping the class	
Teach children the class routines	
Parents	
Give feedback to parents about their child's behaviour – let them know about the good days as well as the bad ones	

What do you think . . .

... the school behaviour policy helps or hinders you? In a new school, find out about the policy. How was it developed, did both staff and pupils have an input? How is it used during lessons in your department or across your age phase? Are rewards used just as much consequences? Do the pupils value the rewards? Is it possible to be truly consistent in the way consequences are given?

Problem

How do you manage a serious incident such as a fight or an aggressive pupil?

Solution

Fortunately, these situations are rare in the classroom. As a trainee, there will always be a mentor or host teacher nearby to help you to manage more challenging situations. Most schools have an 'on call' system where a senior member of staff is available when needed. Activate this, or send a reliable pupil to get help. Keep calm and give assertive instructions; if these are ignored, remember your responsibility is for the safety of the pupils and in some situations it will be appropriate to direct the rest of the class outside the classroom. All teachers have 'the power to use reasonable force to prevent pupils committing an offence, injuring themselves or others, or damaging property, and to maintain good order and discipline in the classroom' (DfE, 2012) and you may need to use this to restrain a pupil from hurting themselves or others. (See Chapter 3 regarding physical contact with pupils.)

Recommended reading

Department for Education (DfE) (2012) *Ensuring Good Behaviour in Schools*. London: DfE.

Department for Education and Skills (DfES) (2004) *The National Strategies: Behaviour and Attendance Toolkit*. London: DfES.

Dix, P. (2010) *The Essential Guide to Taking Care of Behaviour*, 2nd edn. Harlow: Pearson Education.

Hook, P. and Vass, A. (2000) *Confident Classroom Leadership*. London: David Fulton.

Powell, S. and Tod, J. (2004) A systematic review of how theories explain learning behaviour in school contexts, in *Research Evidence in Education Library*. London: EPPI-Centre, Social Science Research Unit, Institution of Education.

Shelton, F. and Brownhill, S. (2008) *Effective Behaviour Management in the Primary Classroom*. Maidenhead: Open University Press.

Taylor, C. (2011) *Getting the Simple Things Right: Charlie Taylor's Behaviour Checklists*. London: DfE.

5 Managing a classroom

Links to Teachers' Standards

Standards Part One: Teaching
Standards Group 2: Effective management of a classroom will promote good progress and outcomes by pupils
Standards Group 5: Differentiated approaches to learning

Introduction

Behaviour management and classroom management are terms that often are used interchangeably. There is a relationship between the terms because for your lessons to run smoothly, you will need to have secure behaviour management skills. However, classroom management is broader. It relates to the physical environment and the management of groups, noise and transitions to promote learning. Effective classroom management relies on you being able to pre-empt problems by thinking carefully about how you organise both the teaching space and pupils. You will get better at this with experience and you will pick up tips from colleagues. An efficient classroom runs like a well-oiled machine but this does not happen by itself.

An effective learning environment plays a significant role in enhancing pupils' learning. Your classroom should be inviting and stimulating so that pupils want to come in and learn. Displays of pupils' work and photographs to show its production should feature in classrooms in all phases of education. Observations of teaching focus sharply on pupil progress. You therefore need to make such progress visible and explicit in the classroom so that it is obvious that your pupils have learnt something new.

The learning environment in the Early Years Foundation Stage

High-quality play should underpin all learning in EYFS. Children should be presented with a range of types of play, including sand and water play, role play, transactional play, construction play and physical play. Mark-making areas can facilitate children's development in literacy, and mathematics areas can provide children with opportunities to explore number, shape, space and measures. Creative areas will encourage children to experiment with paint, collage, drawing, printing and textiles. A malleable area can encourage the development of both creative thinking and physical development, while reading areas should promote children's interest and engagement with a range of text types, including narrative, non-fiction and poetry.

The early years classroom should be a lively, busy place of learning and the learning environment should foster active learning. Very young children learn by doing. The various areas should be labelled using words and graphics and resources should be stored in labelled containers accessible to the children. Young children should be taught how to access resources independently and the labelled storage systems will help them to return the resources to the correct place.

Some of the learning that takes place in the various areas will be structured in that children will be given specific tasks to do. At other times, the play may be unstructured and children will take the learning in their own direction. Play areas can be used for both child-initiated and adult-led tasks. The resources for adult-led tasks can be placed in the play areas for pupils to access independently.

Children should be provided with opportunities to move freely between areas but you will need to find a way of limiting how many children use a specific area at a specific time. Some settings use coloured bands positioned next to the area and when all the bands have been used up, the area is designated as 'full'. Some teachers place a limit on how many areas children can access in a specific session. For example, children may be asked to select to work between two areas, ensuring that they persist with the tasks in those areas, thus adding depth to the learning. Pupil engagement in learning is limited if children do not persist with self-chosen activities.

In many Foundation Stage settings, while the children are engaged in child-initiated play, the teacher and/or teaching assistant may choose to work with specific groups of children or individuals on adult-led tasks. Alternatively, they may choose to support children's own initiated play in the play areas by playing alongside them, interacting with them and developing the pupils' language and thinking.

The outdoor environment is critical in EYFS. Some children prefer to work outside and therefore teachers may well provide reading areas, writing areas and mathematics areas outside. The outdoors provides children with the opportunity to learn about literacy and numeracy on a larger scale and it is a fantastic space for children to make dens! Teachers may also create planting areas for the children to learn about growth. Children should have the opportunity to move between the indoors and outdoors but this will depend on staffing because pupils working in the outdoors need to be supervised.

The environment should be print and number rich. Key vocabulary, captions and sentences should be displayed both indoors and outdoors. In addition, number lines, numerals and shape names should be displayed. Key questions should be positioned next to the play areas so that adults supporting child-initiated play know what questions to ask to extend learning. Key vocabulary should also be displayed so that adults know which words to emphasise as they play alongside pupils.

The play areas should be changed frequently to reflect children's interests and they should be enhanced to link with the class theme or topic.

The learning environment in the primary school

Throughout the primary school, working walls are a useful way of facilitating pupils' learning. Most teachers create one for literacy and one for mathematics, and these are changed frequently so that they relate to the strand that is being taught. You should make reference to the working walls during your lessons and children should use the working walls to support their learning during their lessons.

A mathematics working wall might include:

- Key mathematical vocabulary that is being taught.
- A worked example of a mathematical problem.
- Examples of how the strand of mathematics is applied to everyday life.
- Examples of pupils' mathematical recording.

A literacy working wall might include:

- An example of the text type (genre) that pupils are being taught or examples of the text type at different levels.
- This should be annotated to draw attention to the structural and language features of the text type.
- An example of a planning framework or writing frame.
- Vocabulary choices that relate to the text type.
- Examples of pupils' own plans for writing.
- Examples of pupils' finished work.

Working walls do not need to be neat and tidy and work does not need to be mounted. They support your teaching and the pupils' learning. Pupils can add new vocabulary or questions during their lessons. Working walls are one of the tools for learning that pupils can use to support their learning in a lesson. You might provide your learners with other tools for learning, including:

- number lines or hundred squares
- dictionaries, word mats, alphabet strips
- access to ICT
- spelling rules
- grapheme charts.

The learning environment in the secondary school

Pupils in secondary schools still enjoy seeing their work on display. Consider how you might adopt the principles of working walls to your own subject. Stimulus displays could be created with key facts about a topic. Definitions of subject terminology and key questions could be displayed for pupils to answer. Depending on the subject that you teach, you could include worked examples of how to solve a specific problem.

Pupils in this age group have a heightened sense of fairness, so it is important that equal prominence is given to different levels of work. Only showing the 'best' tends to make displays sterile. It is essential that any work that pupils attempt, where they have put in an effort, should be valued, and being displayed in a classroom setting is one way that this can be demonstrated.

Celebrating pupils' efforts in this way raises self-esteem and finished work should be accompanied with a name label so that everyone can relate the work to a person. During the year you should ensure that all pupils have their work on display and you should celebrate pupils' efforts as well as the outcomes.

One way to involve pupils is to take questions at the start of a topic or unit of work. These could be written on Post-it® notes and stuck on the wall. At the end of a topic, pupils can return to these questions and record their answers on different coloured notes. This could also be done using a mind-mapping format.

Managing noise

You will need to find a noise level that you can tolerate and that is conducive to effective learning. Pupils will not be able to concentrate if the classroom is too noisy. You might find it useful to use a 'noise meter'. A sliding arrow indicates if the noise is okay, slightly loud or unacceptable. You can move the arrow up or down during the lesson so that pupils can monitor their own noise levels. You will need to consider the consequences that you will implement if the noise becomes unacceptable. Some children respond well to calm music being played during the lesson. Involve the pupils in discussions about what they consider to be a suitable working noise level and ask them to think about what the consequences might be if the class becomes too noisy. Remember that not all noise is bad noise. Pupils may be talking about their learning and collaborating, which is what good learners do!

Managing transitions

Transitions are times when pupils move from one task to another and they can potentially be disruptive. The trick that you need to master is to make them really slick and smooth, so that there is no wasted learning time within lessons.

Managing support

Effective use of support staff means they make a striking impact on pupils' progress at all stages of the lesson. They will need a clear role during all parts of the lesson. They could make observations of specific pupils by noting their responses or they could sit next to them to keep them focused. If the lesson content is not appropriate for specific pupils, the teaching assistant could provide individual intervention away from the main teaching input.

Managing the classroom layout

Once you start your teaching career, you will need to make decisions about how to organise the furniture in your classroom. During your initial teacher training, you are not likely to get the opportunity to do this because you will be walking into a classroom that is already set up. Your layout should be flexible if possible and linked to the type of learning planned.

Group work

Organising tables into groups is common in most primary classrooms because most teachers believe that pupils work best when they collaborate. Vygotsky emphasised the role of social interaction and language in promoting learning. Consider how large you want the groups to be. Groups of between four to six pupils are ideal but any more than this could be too large and lead to distractions. Pupils need adequate space to work, so try to ensure that all pupils have an equal amount of space. Consider **how** you are going to group your pupils – by ability, mixed ability, friendship, gender, etc.

Flexibility

Generally in primary schools, pupils are organised into ability groups for literacy and mathematics. Using ability groups enables you to target the needs of each group by setting differentiated tasks. The drawback to ability grouping is that pupils are quick to work out which group is the brightest group and which group is working at a lower stage of development, even if you never refer to this. Keep your groups flexible, as pupils can make greater or less progress than expected so may need to switch groups during the year. Recognise that pupils may demonstrate good ability in certain areas of mathematics or literacy and lesser ability in other areas of the same subject. A pupil may struggle to solve calculations but may be brilliant at shape, space and measures; a pupil may struggle with writing but be a really fluent reader. In such instances, operate flexible systems that allow for pupils to switch groups within the same subject.

The children also need opportunities to work with different pupils, so use mixed-ability grouping some of the time, even within literacy and mathematics. This will enable more able pupils to support the learning of others. This is an application of Vygotsky's concept of the *zone of proximal development*, where learners are aided to reach higher levels of knowledge, skills and understanding with the support of a more able other.

In the EYFS, main teaching input often takes place with pupils seated on the floor. Pupils then move to tables to complete tasks. As children progress through primary school they are often seated at tables for the main teaching input and for the tasks. By secondary school, much of this flexibility seems to have been lost, but this does not need to be the case. Arranging tables in groups is useful if you want pupils to work collaboratively. Give each pupil a different role within the group and over time allow them to take on different roles.

Paired work

Give careful consideration to how you pair pupils, for example, by friendship pairs or ability. The pairings could be changed during the year to enable pupils to work with others. Paired work may minimise noise and disruption but pupils will still talk to others sitting in front and behind.

Horseshoe

Organising the tables into a horseshoe ensures that all the pupils can see you and each other during the lesson. This is particularly beneficial for facilitating discussion. Consider your own positioning within the horseshoe arrangement. You may wish to sit or stand at the front or you might choose to position yourself within the horseshoe to minimise the power dynamics between you and your pupils.

Adapt your approaches to classroom management to different groups and ages of pupils. Strategies that work for one group may be ineffective with another. Your classroom has a number of elements that need managing – space, people, resources and pupil groups. Ultimately, no one method of grouping pupils is perfect. Each method has its strengths and drawbacks. It seems sensible to be flexible and to operate different types of grouping arrangements to fulfil different purposes. Sometimes you may want to move all the tables to the side and stack the chairs to create an open teaching space. This is particularly useful if you want to run a drama/role-play activity or even for organising class debates. Sometimes you may want a circle (nowhere to hide).

Managing your groupings carefully and providing your pupils with tools for learning in the classroom will help to minimise any potential problems.

Conclusion

Good learners come straight into the classroom and they are ready to learn. Good learners also ask questions and persist with tasks even when they are challenging. Your pupils need to know what it means to be a good learner. They need to understand the characteristics displayed by good learners and it is your responsibility to praise them when they demonstrate these characteristics. Good learners collaborate with others and do not immediately ask a teacher when they encounter a problem. You cannot assume that your pupils will understand what good learning looks like. But you could ask them what they think are the characteristics of good learners and less effective learners. Once they 'hook' into this you can create a display about the attributes of good learners. They are more likely to demonstrate the characteristics of good learning if they are aware of them in the first place.

Train your pupils to come straight into class and get straight into learning. Have a starter activity for them to do immediately when they come into the room. This could relate to prior learning. Keep it short and then get on with the new learning. Passive learners are not good learners. You need to encourage your pupils to talk to each other about their learning, to debate, to ask questions, to challenge, and so on. A quiet classroom is seldom a learning classroom!

What we have learned

- The learning environment plays a critical role in supporting learning
- Transitions need to be carefully managed
- Grouping arrangements need to be flexible for different purposes

Advice and ideas (1)

The use of plastic 'assessment for learning' cups (red, amber, green cups) helps monitor learning. Each pupil is provided with three cups. When they do not need help they select the green cup and put it in front of them. When they are struggling but persisting with a problem they select the amber cup, and when they are completely stuck they select the red cup. The teacher then knows instantly which pupils need further support and this stops pupils becoming disengaged. It also prevents the pupils from having to publicly declare that they need help because they do not need to put their hand up.

Advice and ideas (2)

Find a 'hook' that will draw children into learning. This needs to be done at the beginning of the lesson and its purpose is to make your pupils want to learn. Literally anything could be used as a hook. Examples include:

- a short clip of a film
- an unusual object or a collection of objects, e.g. objects belonging to a person from history
- using ICT to take children into a different environment, e.g. immersive spaces
- a letter sent from a story character to the class
- using Post-it® notes for them to record their ideas
- using an image
- doing something active
- using video conferencing to create a live discussion with someone in another place.

What do you think . . .

. . . that you need a chair and table for each child in the Foundation Stage? Is it necessary for every child to have a place? Is a teacher's desk necessary? Why?

Problem

One problem that you may encounter is how to provide focused guided teaching to one group of pupils while at the same time keeping the rest of the class productively engaged so that they do not interrupt you.

Solution

Use a traffic light system to plan the tasks. This works in the following way:

- **Red activities.** These are those tasks that cannot be completed without adult supervision and guidance. If there is only one adult in the classroom, you may have to limit these kinds of tasks to one group. If you are working with a teaching assistant, you may be able to plan two groups.

- **Amber activities.** These are tasks that pupils can generally work on independently with occasional guidance from an adult. The adult may be supporting the 'red' tasks but once these pupils reach the point of being able to apply the taught skills independently, the adult will be able to dip in and out of the groups.
- **Green activities.** These are tasks that pupils can work on independently without adult guidance. The tasks may be consolidation activities related to prior learning so that pupils are able to work with little or no supervision.

If you plan too many red activities, all the pupils will need adult support at the same time and you will end up servicing the class rather than teaching them.

Try not to spread yourself too thinly so that all the groups need your support at the same time. Queues of pupils waiting to see a teacher could be an indication of poor classroom management.

Recommended reading

Allal, L. and Ducrey, G. (2000) Assessment of or in the zone of proximal development, *Learning and Instruction*, 10 (2): 137–52.

Roberts, H. (2012) *Oops! Helping Children Learn Accidently*. Carmarthen: Independent Thinking Press.

Vygotsky, L.S. (1978) *Mind and Society: The Development of Higher Psychological Processes*. Cambridge, MA: Harvard University Press.

CHAPTER 6

Planning lessons

What this chapter covers

- Lesson planning in the context of medium- and longer-term planning

- Starters and plenaries

- Learning objectives and outcomes

- Teacher exposition

- Approaches to active learning

Links to Teachers' Standards

Standards Part One: Teaching
Standards Group 3: Demonstrate good subject and curriculum knowledge
Standards Group 4: Plan and teach well-structured lessons

Introduction

Planning teaching and learning activities that are engaging, purposeful and appropriate to meet the needs of the pupils is fundamental to becoming a successful teacher. It is an intellectual and creative task that draws on a deep understanding of how children learn; subject knowledge and pedagogy; of what progress looks like in each subject;

and of any statutory curriculum and assessment requirements that the pupils are required to meet.

Each lesson needs a sense of purpose and it is important that we share this purpose with the pupils. They need to understand where they are going on the journey and why; this helps them to be committed to getting there! Lessons have several key components that are structured carefully in order to maximise pupils' engagement in learning:

- The lesson starts with an activity to whet their appetite and to connect current to prior learning.
- Sometimes you will need to model a new skill, or explain a new concept through this 'teacher exposition'. This skill can be practised and honed to have real impact in helping pupils to develop their understanding.
- As explained further in Chapter 7, pupils need to grapple with the new information for themselves; to investigate, manipulate, practise, contextualise, try in different contexts, seek alternatives, problematise, find solutions for and refine if they are to be able to remember it, use it and build on it in subsequent lessons.
- You will want pupils to demonstrate their new learning and understanding during the lesson, as this will help you to decide on the next stage of their development as well as providing an opportunity for you to celebrate success and give feedback (or more accurately, feed-forward) to help them to make further progress.
- Plenary activities consolidate pupils' understanding by helping them to reflect on what they have learned from the activity and during the lesson.

Managing these components is the skill and art of teaching. Knowing when to move on and when the pupils need a little bit more time, asking the right questions to make them think and knowing how to make progress possible for every pupil in a class, these are all aspects that need advance planning, but also you need to be able to think on your feet and be reactive to the pupils' responses if the lesson is going to have pace and real impact.

Learning objectives and outcomes

Different settings have different policies and practices in relation to these, which can be confusing to beginning teachers. To simplify, the learning objective is what you want the pupils to *learn* in the lesson. This might be knowledge based, it might be about acquiring and applying a concept, it might be to do with developing a skill, or it might be about developing attitudes, values or creativity. The confusion comes because it's much easier to write what you want the pupils to *do* rather than what you want them to *learn*.

An example of this might be 'In today's lesson, I want pupils to be able to write a short story'. This is a lesson outcome, not an objective. The outcome is the 'product' of the lesson; it is what pupils can do if they have grasped the learning objective. So, to write meaningful lesson objectives for this lesson, think about the learning that needs to take place if the pupils are going to be able to write a successful short story. This might be about how to develop interesting and believable characters, or it might be about plot construction or about description and scene setting. When you get it right, the learning objectives will dictate completely the learning activities that you need to plan for the lesson.

Learning outcomes are often written at three levels:

- What will the most able pupils be able to do?
- What will all the pupils be able to do?
- And what will the majority be able to do?

Think carefully about this, it should be about the level of understanding, rather than a case of being able to do more – the *quality* of the outcome rather than quantity. During the lesson, build in opportunities to share with pupils what 'quality' looks like, and the evidence you are seeking. When pupils know what they are aiming for, you can use peer and self-assessment to help them to refine and improve their work (see Chapter 10). Planning and thinking about this before the lesson also helps you to make powerful interventions that support individual pupils' learning and to stretch and challenge them, because you understand what they need to do to improve their work.

Lesson starters

A good starter sets the tone for the whole of the lesson. It needs careful planning to get the class settled and working productively as quickly as possible. It is prime learning time and is often wasted with the register, collecting homework, giving out equipment, admonishments for lateness, and so on. A good starter activity can capture pupils' interest and engage them immediately. Routine is important; pupils should anticipate that they ought begin to work as soon as they arrive. To plan an effective starter, think about its purpose. In a new topic, it might be that you need to find out what the pupils already know, or in a subsequent lesson, you will want to jog their memory in order to make connections with previous learning. You may want to use the task to introduce them to a new concept in order to give them an opportunity to investigate, speculate or cogitate, or you might use this part of the lesson to practise a particular skill on a 'little and often' basis.

The most important thing is that *all* pupils are engaged in the task. Being 'engaged' is different to being 'occupied'; engagement means that they are actively involved – thinking, making decisions and definitely not passive. A starter activity is a short task, no more than 7–10 minutes' duration, so although it should require pupils to think at a deep level, it needs to be immediately accessible for everyone. Encourage engagement by making expectations clear, for example, 'each pair needs to decide on the most important aspect in three minutes', and also by intervening appropriately to ask a challenging question at the right moment, or by asking a pupil what they think in order to draw them into the conversation.

Often starter activities are resource heavy; they may involve photographs, manipulatives (things to label, match, group, rank, sequence, complete) or problem-solving activities. Plan carefully how these will be distributed and collected in order to keep the pace moving and to ensure that you do not constantly have to remake your resources. It is important to plan for variety; any activity, no matter how active, if used too often loses its impact, but above all remember that the starter is a learning opportunity, it needs to support the learning objectives for the lesson.

Teacher exposition

There is a balance to be struck in a lesson between teacher talk and pupil activity. It also has to be planned carefully in advance so that pupils can truly understand or visualise the new idea. To make an explanation interesting and to hold pupils' attention, it must be clear, concise and logical. Think carefully about how you can connect it to their current understanding and experience through the use of models, analogies, examples and non-examples. So in music, a simple analogy for an ascending scale might be walking up the stairs. You might grab pupils' attention by using a prop, or making an unusual connection, or through the use of humour. Clarity comes from thinking carefully about sequence in the explanation and from the signposting of important aspects, for example 'This is the most important thing you need to remember …'. You can also plan appropriate questions to check pupils' understanding, and challenge and engage them by asking them to predict the next stage, or what might happen in different contexts.

A different type of explanation is needed when the issue involves developing or improving a process or skill, such as teaching how to make a slide for a microscope in science, to do a subtraction in maths or to improvise a twelve bar blues melody in music. Showing or demonstrating how to do these things is not enough; playing a blues improvisation and saying to pupils 'this is how you do it' is not very helpful. In order to learn, pupils need to understand the thought processes and the 'inner knowledge' used to complete the task successfully. For example, as a more experienced musician, the teacher knows which 'blue' notes to add to make the improvisation sound authentic; what sort of rhythms to play and the musical response to the backing. To improve pupils' improvisations, this 'hidden' knowledge must be shared with pupils. This is good modelling. To plan successful models, identify your thought processes and the prior knowledge you access in order to complete the task successfully. Then practise completing the task while explaining these so that when you do it in a lesson, it is slick, well-structured and engaging for the pupils. It is also helpful to anticipate where the pupils are likely to struggle or to have misconceptions, and to plan how you might provide opportunities for pupils to ask questions for clarification.

Differentiation

During the lesson it is vital that pupils have opportunities to actively engage in independent learning in order to understand and make sense of new information (see Chapter 7). Differentiation is the means by which we ensure that pupils have the appropriate levels of support and challenge to guarantee that they *all* make good progress during the lesson. There are many ways of doing this:

- **Differentiation by task:** open-ended tasks that facilitate engagement at different levels, graduated tasks, different tasks, further challenges, tasks that support different learning preferences, choice of task outcomes, must/should/could, different amounts of time to complete activities.
- **Differentiation by support:** resources with texts of different depth, breadth and difficulty, scaffolding such as writing frames, careful pairing and grouping of pupils, integrating the use of support staff, teacher interventions, independent learning activities.
- **Differentiated questioning, feedback and targets:** open and closed questions, higher-order questioning and thinking, wait time, individual targets based on prior learning, targeted interventions to develop specific skills, devising own challenges.

During this part of the lesson, teacher intervention is the most powerful way of helping pupils to progress further. Your observations, questions and conversations with pupils can support and challenge their thinking while they are working and you can look for teaching opportunities to share with the whole class. Carefully plan the layout of the classroom to ensure that it is appropriate to support the tasks that the pupils are doing. Flexible seating arrangements are the best; for example, a double horseshoe shape supports class discussion, individual, paired and small group work. Make sure that the resources needed to complete the tasks are well organised and centrally available for pupils to collect as they need them.

Early Years Foundation Stage

In the early years, you need to pay as much attention to planning your learning environment as planning your lessons. This is because most of the learning that takes place in the early years is through play. Plan stimulating play areas with resources that engage pupils' interests. Regularly enhance these areas based on children's interests. Also provide opportunities for pupils to apply the learning they have been introduced to in adult-led tasks in their own independent learning through their play. Create stimulating exploratory areas for children to investigate using their senses, thus developing their curiosity. Provide attractive reading areas and exciting role-play areas as well as opportunities for sand, water, construction and malleable play. In the early years, learning is not confined to adult-led teaching opportunities. Children should be given just as much opportunity to pursue their own independent learning through their play.

Demonstrating learning

This part of the lesson is where the pupils demonstrate their learning through the learning outcomes. This might be a performance, a piece of writing, a poster, a presentation, a model, a piece of artwork, a design, a demonstration, a reasoned argument or answers to problems. Ensuring that you have a good variety of the types of outcome required over time will help to maintain pupils' interest and even more so if the pupils have some choice in the way they present their learning. This is an important opportunity for feedback and formative assessment. To help pupils to refine their work, opportunities should be made available for 'taking stock' against the success criteria through teacher intervention and peer and self-assessment during the activity phase of the lesson. Towards the end of the lesson, celebrate success and put the learning into context.

Plenaries

Plenary activities are intended to summarise and pull together the learning that has taken place during an activity or during the lesson. Such activities can provide a transition to the next stage of the learning and consolidate and extend pupils' understanding of the learning objective. They highlight what has been learned and encourage thinking about how it might be applied in different contexts. The best plenaries are an active part of the lesson, planned in a similar way to a starter activity with appropriate levels of challenge, pace and engagement, focusing on pupils reflecting on their learning. Examples include:

- '3 Roles'. Divide the class into groups of three. One group member describes what they've done, one reflects on how they did it and the other describes how the learning can be used in other situations.
- '321 Review'. Pupils write on six Post-it® notes, one thing they already knew, two things they still want to find out and three things they have learned.
- 'What if?'. The teacher poses a series of 'what if?' questions: What if we hadn't done today's lesson? What if you weren't allowed to know what we've learnt today? What if everything I've told you today is false?
- 'Just a minute'. In small groups, one pupil has to speak about the topic covered for one minute. At the first repetition, pause or mistake, another pupil takes over.
- 'Conversion'. Ask the pupils to convert the material used in the lesson into a different format, such as a concept into a flow diagram or a description into five key words.

Conclusion

Individual lesson planning comes at the end of much deeper reflection and organisation of a long-term plan of sequences of lessons which ensure pupils' progress over time. Imagine each lesson as a step of a walk on a much longer expedition; you have to know where you are going in order to get there in the most efficient way possible. When you first start teaching, it's likely that the long-term plan or scheme of work (the expedition) and the medium-term plans or units of work (the walk) will be planned already. If you are to plan and teach successful lessons (the steps), you need to have a fundamental understanding of the expected progress of the pupils and the rationale that underpins the decisions about the order of events in the units and in the scheme of work.

The tasks you choose are key to success. You can use a variety of tasks to teach one learning objective so the task simply provides a motivating context for pupils to learn something new. Both you and your pupils should be clear on what new learning will emerge from the task(s). You first need to consider what you want your pupils to learn and only when you are clear about this should you think about designing a task to enable them to learn it.

What we have learned

- The key components of lessons
- How to plan active learning experiences that engage and motivate pupils
- Each lesson is part of a longer unit of work, which, in turn, is part of a well-organised longer-term scheme of work
- All the components are focused on pupils' progression in the subject over time.

Advice and ideas (1)

Using Anderson and Krathwohl's (2001) *Taxonomy for Learning, Teaching and Assessing* to help you to devise learning tasks is a powerful way to develop activities that are challenging and engaging. Engaging pupils in analysing, evaluating and creating involves them thinking at a much deeper level than activities which rely on knowledge recall. *All* pupils can engage in higher-order thinking, and skilful questioning by the teacher can ensure that pupils are appropriately stretched and challenged throughout.

Advice and ideas (2)

Collaborative working is a strategy that can help to engage, motivate, challenge and support pupils during all phases of the lesson, but successful group work requires careful preparation. First, decide on the type of group – friendship to create an unthreatening way of working, ability to challenge pupils at particular levels, mixed ability to support different levels of understanding, or random to build pupils' experiences of working with different pupils. Decisions about the size of group depend on the task: smaller groups (3–4) work best when there are decisions to be made and you expect an end product; larger groups (5–7) are useful for brainstorming and discussion-based activities but are likely to need a chair or leader. Assigning roles to individuals in groups is a good way to ensure everyone's participation and engagement.

What do you think . . .

... successful learning looks like? To gain an understanding of the planning process, some fundamental questions need to be answered:

- What does successful learning in my subject look like?
- What does 'understanding' mean in my subject?
- What skills and attributes do the pupils have when they get better at my subject?

The answers to these questions will give you a vision of the 'finishing line' and help you to plan the 'expedition' to get there. The overriding principle is one of purpose; each unit of work, each lesson, each activity must have the purpose of helping *all* pupils to achieve their potential as a learner in the subject.

Problem

When groups are working independently on creative thinking and active tasks, what is the role of the teacher?

Solution

Knowing when to intervene and when to observe is a crucial skill; too much intervention and you can stifle creativity, too little and the pupils can be 'lost' and slow to make progress. Even when the pupils appear to be stuck, you need to resist the urge to tell them what to do. Instead, ask questions to help them to generate their own solutions: 'What would happen if?', 'Why have you decided?', 'How can you?', 'Do you agree with?' Observing the group as they work is a real opportunity for you to gain a deeper awareness of the pupils' understanding of the topic, which will help you to plan the next stage of their learning.

Recommended reading

Anderson, L.W. and Krathwohl, D.R. (eds) (2001) *A Taxonomy for Learning, Teaching, and Assessing: A Revision of Bloom's Taxonomy of Educational Objectives*. New York: Longman.

Ginnis, P. (2002) *The Teacher's Toolkit*. Carmarthen: Crown House Publishing.

Smith, A. (1998) *Accelerated Learning in Practice: Brain-based Methods for Accelerating Motivation and Achievement*. Stafford: Network Educational.

CHAPTER 7

Pupil-centred learning

What this chapter covers

- The importance of putting the pupil at the centre of the teaching/learning axis

- Beginning to understand how pupils learn

- Developing pupil-centred learning

- Considering different types of learning

- Teaching pupils whose first language is not English

Links to Teachers' Standards

Standards Part One: Teaching
Standards Group 2: Promote good progress and outcomes by pupils by having prior knowledge of attainment and building on this
Standards Group 5: Pupil-centred learning is a key way to demonstrate that you have adapted teaching to respond to the strengths and needs of all pupils

Introduction

Learning that has the pupils at the centre is key to ensuring that it is the pupils who are doing the work – and thus the learning – and not the teacher. It is learning that should be the focus in the classroom, not teaching, and learning that should be the outcome of a lesson, not knowledge. There is a difference between learning and instruction, with the latter not necessarily resulting in the former. Ivan Illich (1971: 24) claims that

> … learning is the human activity which least needs manipulation by others. Most learning is not the result of instruction. It is rather the result of unhampered participation in a meaningful setting.

You need, therefore, to consider what your role really is in the classroom, and how you can encourage real or 'deep' learning, which has the pupil at its centre, rather than just rote learning of knowledge.

What do children learn?

Even in a state sector that proscribes the content of a central national curriculum, it is always disappointing to hear a pupil (or a teacher, for that matter) making the comment when asked why they are learning a particular topic that it is 'because it is for the examination'. These are pupils that are being taught 'content' because that content is centrally dictated (remember that outside the LEA-supported sector, at academies and 'free' schools, the National Curriculum does not apply) but who are not really 'learning' anything. As an inspirational teacher you must develop learning, rather than concentrating on the recall of knowledge. Knowing how to fly an aeroplane is not the same as doing it; think who you would prefer to be at the controls!

Teacher-centred learning

In the traditional, teacher-centred approach, the emphasis is squarely on outcomes; learning is measured by what the pupil can reproduce. The pupil is considered to be an empty (or almost empty) vessel into which knowledge can be poured. In this system, the knowledge content is set centrally and externally, by examination board or government curriculum, so that, whatever the local needs or circumstances, all learn the same things. Thus the pupil remembers, but does not necessarily understand or see the relevance. Pupils have facts, but don't quite know what to do with them. What good are the colours of the rainbow, the order of the planets, the kings and queens of history or the list of longest rivers? What use are passages memorised from famous speeches or 'set' books of literature, with no context or purpose? Laurie Lee's 1959 novel *Cider with Rosie*, set in post-First World War Gloucestershire, might have been one of your set books. Lee paints a vivid picture of early twentieth-century primary education. He describes the village school and, crucially, what it taught:

> Every child in the valley crowding there, remained till he was fourteen years old, then was presented to the working field or factory, with nothing in his head more burdensome than a few mnemonics, a jumbled list of wars, and a dreamy image of the world's geography.

The way by which the success of this approach is measured is to train the pupil in retention, so that the knowledge can be poured back out, preferably in oppressive conditions and under a strict time limit. In addition, in the worst examples of teacher-centred learning, all pupils are considered to be at the same level, so little or no attempt is made to simplify work for the less able, or to stretch the more gifted.

Pupil-centred learning

In pupil-centred learning, the focus moves away from the teacher and on to the pupil. The ideal ratio in a lesson is probably something like 80:20. That is, 80% of the time the pupils are on task, working, actively learning; 20% of the time the teacher is giving instructions, clarifying points and correcting mistakes and misunderstandings. Active learning is inextricably linked to pupil-centred learning. The elements that make a pupil-centred learning experience 'fly' (see illustration) are:

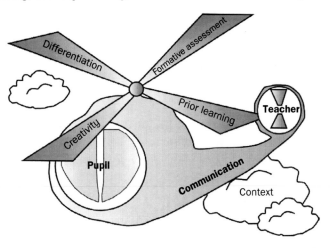

- **Contextualisation.** Pupils are provided with, or create their own, context for the learning. This gives the learning purpose and helps the pupil to understand its application and thus to apply it in novel situations. Employability skills – being able to apply learning in a work situation – are a subset of this.
- **Communication.** There are dialogues between pupils and teacher and between pupil and pupil, so there is both communication and cross-fertilisation. Learning becomes much more of a social activity, with teacher facilitation, and pupils working in pairs and in groups. This also encourages problem-solving approaches and self-learning by pupils. Peer-to-peer communication has value, and the social setting (behaviours, attitudes) is also being learned.
- **Prior learning.** Pupils have knowledge of the world and some experience of it, however young they may be. Your teaching should start from a position of 'what do they know already?', so questioning is of paramount importance (see Chapter 8). Prior learning is used to establish a baseline from which progress can be made. Without checking on it, the teacher runs the risk of demotivating pupils by merely covering knowledge and skills that they already possess.
- **Formative assessment** is used in preference to summative assessment. This is linked with the teacher's role as facilitator rather than instructor. The

teacher's role becomes to encourage, to praise what is correct or imaginative, or innovative, or which shows a thought process being used, or shows effort – criteria are many and varied. A major role is to question, to test and embed understanding, and to encourage further progress by indicating possible 'directions of travel'.

- **Differentiation.** Not all children have the same ability (or the same prior knowledge or experiences), so you need to provide different 'routes' to your chosen destination (see Chapter 6). For each lesson or series of lessons, decide what the underlying essential learning is going to be for each pupil and how each can best achieve this. In addition, establish further targets for the more able and possibly more complex or demanding tasks, and plan appropriate support and interventions for weaker pupils.

- **Creativity.** Actively engaging teaching relies on creative approaches so, for example, try to introduce something unusual to your lesson to promote interest – it doesn't matter if it's an artefact, an activity or a context. Encourage children to use their imaginations and to be creative, as this improves confidence. If the balance of creativity and innovation is right (Donovan, 2005), coupled with activities and exercises that reflect what pupils say helps them to learn, and if trainees develop a reflective approach, rooted in teaching creatively, then both teaching and learning are more effective.

Why do children learn?

To combine these building blocks successfully in a classroom requires the teacher to introduce one more element, and that is the motivation to learn. Think of teaching a pupil, at any age in primary or secondary school, in the same way as a parent thinks of teaching a very young child. There is coaxing, there are rewards, there are words of praise and encouragement. There is repetition, simplification of instructions, a slowing down or speeding up of pace as appropriate. This is because the parent recognises that the baby or toddler must learn in order, first, to survive, and second, to progress and grow. The key to effective learning is thus motivation. The child – or pupil – that is motivated to learn will be the one that learns most effectively. Learning that has a purpose is inherently more effective than that which does not. Sometimes that purpose may be of a higher order – maybe I wish to learn to play the piano just to further my own enjoyment – maybe it is more esoteric and I just like to be able to puzzle things out to keep my brain working, but in all cases **wanting** to learn is the key.

Routes to learning

There are different routes to learning, linked to subject matter. If you wanted the child to learn a behaviour (like potty training), then repetition linked to praise is appropriate; if you want the child to learn some useful knowledge, you might demonstrate and instruct. One example could be the parent putting his or her hand near a flame or hot surface and acting 'ow, hot', reinforced with the instruction to stay away from such dangers. Sometimes, as with a skill, it can only be learned by 'doing'. You cannot teach a child to ride a bike from a book. They must make the attempt, learn to balance and (the 7-year-old's rite of passage) get to 'look Mum, no hands!' on their own. And as part of this process they must learn to fail (you can't learn to ride a bicycle without falling off a few times). Parents try to limit the failures by providing scaffolding – a structure for the learning. They gradually increase independence as the skill improves. In learning a skill, the child will also learn to analyse and to solve problems. The main areas of learning are:

- **Knowledge:** delivered through oral or written communication and tested by recall.
- **Motor skills:** these can be 'taught' but must be independently learned, everything from walking to playing a musical instrument or sawing in a straight line.
- **Attitudes and behaviour:** delivered by modelling and demonstration.
- **Intellectual skills:** problem solving, analysis, critical skills, adaptation of learning to novel situations.

You thus need to decide what you are teaching, why pupils might want to learn it, then how you can engage the pupils in the learning. A road map to show the journey that you would like the pupils to take is a useful tool. Do not be afraid to share this with the pupils. It may be summarised in five questions:

- Where are they now? Prior learning discovered through questioning.
- How do I know this? Previous assessments, clear records of progress.
- Where do I want them to be? Differentiated targets so that all can progress.
- How will I help them get there? Methods, delivery, activities, support, context.
- How will I know when they have arrived? Continuing assessment, especially valuing work successfully completed. This then provides the starting point for the next lesson.

Pupil-centred ideas for exercises and activities

Pupils working in pairs or small groups have a range of learning preferences, making such social learning more effective. Pairs should be encouraged to discuss issues and to present work in different ways. One technique is think–pair–share. Each pupil THINKS of a solution or undertakes an activity individually. Each then discusses ideas with his or her partner in a PAIR. They then SHARE with another pair, a small group and finally a group spokesperson shares with the whole class.

In terms of encouraging creativity, pupils can be asked to create poems, raps, pictures, cartoons or role plays so that they can access a range of learning styles. This also helps to encourage pupil ownership of work. If they own the work, they are more likely to value it and therefore more likely to put in effort to produce it. You should reinforce this by ensuring that you value the work yourself and by encouraging peers to do so. Groups can also be encouraged to share their work in different ways.

Individuals should be encouraged to be self-pacing, and intermediate targets should be introduced so that each can succeed. Pupils should understand that they have a responsibility for their own learning. This will be linked to the motivation supplied by you. You may also use self-assessment techniques to encourage progress. The job of the teacher is often to use facilitation to provide the stepping-stones to make the targets more attainable and the praise to recognise effort and progress.

Diversity and inclusion

All pupils must be included in your lessons. It is not just different abilities that should drive a differentiated approach, but all the other differences that may be present in the classroom. These include obvious differences such as gender and ethnicity, together with:

- physical differences such as sight, hearing and mobility
- emotional, behavioural and learning needs
- social, cultural, family and religious differences
- English as an alternative language (EAL).

The population of classrooms in the UK continues to become more and more diverse. Diversity should be celebrated and used as a way to encourage behaviours of tolerance and acceptance. So, for example, at primary level you could base lessons on different religious festivals, introduce stories from different cultures and ensure that differences in dress, food or habits are understood and appreciated. In the secondary school, you should not rely on personal education or form time to deal with differences but instead try to celebrate them within your lessons.

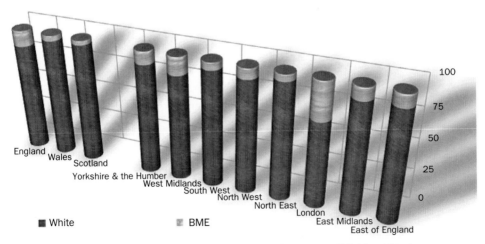

Source: Adapted from ONS: Office for National Statistics (2012 online).

English as an alternative language

Department for Education data (DFE, 2010) says that out of the 7.4 million pupils educated in the non-fee-paying education sector (4.1 million primary pupils, 3.3 million secondary pupils), approximately 656,000 primary pupils and 382,800 secondary pupils do not have English as their first language. You are therefore extremely likely to teach one or more pupils that fall into this category. In terms of EAL, there will be specialist colleagues available to help you, but you can do much yourself, first, by understanding the process of second language learning and, second, by valuing the second languages in the classroom.

Being a beginner in English does not equate to an inability to be able to learn. Often children (especially refugees from war zones) have been denied education, so you do not know their potential. Many new arrivals will also pass through a 'silent' stage, lacking the confidence to communicate. You should prepare key words in the pupils' own language and use visual clues to support your teaching. Technology can also provide translation software (be wary of this, and check it both ways). A 'buddy' system with an English speaker helps to build confidence and language skills. Specialist teaching assistants should be involved in planning. You need to ensure that they have a role to support learning, not provide an easy conversational route in the pupil's language.

Conclusion

You will be told that there are many theories around pupil learning 'styles' and referred to Skinner, Kolb, Honey and Mumford, and Gardner among others. You will need to study what these psychologists and educationalists have to say, but then will need to formulate your own theories as to what is effective in your classroom, with your pupils. Chief among these ways is the notion that pupils may prefer to learn through visual, aural or kinaesthetic routes (VAK). In other words, some like primarily to see, some to hear, some to do. In many cases, however, this depends more on what is being learned (subject and skills area) rather than any preferred style and pupils will change their learning preferences according to the subject, context and activity.

What we have learned

- That teacher-centred 'learning' is mostly sterile
- That learners need to be motivated
- That there are different routes to learning
- That you need to adapt teaching to different learners
- To be aware of and plan for differentiation, inclusion and EAL

Advice and ideas (1)

Sharing information and results between groups can be a powerful tool, but needs to be managed. The most common way is to appoint a spokesperson to feed back to the class. Other methods include:

- **Peer assessment.** Groups assess the work of other groups, using agreed criteria. This can be done by awarding points, or smiley faces, along with positive criticism.
- **Ambassadors.** Each group appoints an ambassador, who visits each other group (country) in turn (one ambassador at a time per country) and shares ideas, findings, discussion points.
- **Whistle stop.** Groups move in one direction around the room on the whistle (or music), spending a short amount of time (a) reading/looking at/assessing what other groups have done and (b) adding missing points/comments/marks. This is active, but quick and controlled.
- **Ideas café.** Large sheets of paper are put on each table as a 'tablecloth'. Groups rotate, adding ideas or views in their own coloured pens.

Advice and ideas (2)

In primary classes, consider how you could provide 'tools for learning' to enable pupils to access the lesson. Children working at lower stages of development in mathematics can be supported with access to number lines, hundred squares, counters, tens and units apparatus, and multilink cubes. Children working at lower stages of development can be supported by access to alphabet mats, spelling mats and dictionaries. There are many more tools for learning but ultimately they help to break down barriers to learning and enable children to access the lesson. In the early years, it is now common for teachers to plan topics and play areas around children's interests.

What do you think . . .

. . . learning is for? The idea of passing knowledge from one generation to another sounds like a philosophy that cannot be questioned. But surely it is what is done with that knowledge that is important. Knowledge in itself is of no use unless the receiver of it can learn how to use it. It is like passing the instructions to make fire from one generation to another in a sealed pot, with no-one ever striking a flint. Surely the purpose of history is empathy; of mathematics problem solving; of language communication through speaking, reading and writing; of economics understanding (and ability to manipulate) systems and markets; of engineering how things work and how we can improve; of science the ability to question, analyse and theorise; of art, music and dance the ability to create, interpret and appreciate; of PE to gain and hone skills. Is there anything that is truly learned without a purpose?

Problem

Sometimes we make learning more difficult without realising it. Consider the barriers to learning that we might accidentally introduce. For example, think about teaching a child to tie a shoelace.

Solution

How many of us realise that we can make this (fairly complicated) knot much harder to learn than it needs to be, by showing the child face-to-face, thus expecting him or her to reverse every action? Think about this when teaching – what barriers are you inadvertently throwing up? These could be psychological – do pupils see you as exercising power over them rather than trying to help them?; have you inadvertently taken up a dominant posture or position? Or they could be embedded in your teaching – are you using vocabulary that is at too high a level?; are you assuming understanding?; are you making bridging links between concepts even before the concepts are clearly understood?

Recommended reading

Donovan, G. (2005) *Teaching 14–19 – Everything You Need to Know About Teaching and Learning Across the Phases.* London: Fulton.

Illich, I. (1971) *Deschooling Society.* New York: Calder & Boyers.

Kyriacou, C. (2009) *Effective Teaching in Schools.* London: Nelson Thornes.

Lee, L. (1959) *Cider with Rosie.* London: Hogarth Press.

Office for National Statistics (ONS) (2012) *Ethnicity and National Identity in England and Wales 2011: Key Statistics for Local Authorities in England and Wales.* Released 11 December. London: ONS.

8 The skill of asking questions

Links to Teachers' Standards

Standards Part One: Teaching
Standards Group 2: Promote good progress and outcomes by pupils by having prior knowledge of attainment and building on this
Standards Group 5: Good questioning shows that you are responding to the strengths and needs of all pupils

Introduction

Questioning is the way by which a teacher checks current knowledge and understanding and, post-learning, that further knowledge and understanding have developed.

Without good questioning, it is impossible to know whether a group, or an individual within a group, is making progress or needs support. It also helps motivate learners, as it encourages them to take part and to be involved in the lesson. The skill of questioning, however, needs to be developed.

Leven and Long (1981) reckoned that teachers asked between 300 and 400 questions a day, but tempered this by also noting that the majority of these were low-level 'knowledge' questions that required simple responses. It is not the number of questions that you ask your pupils that is important, it is the quality of those questions – the reasons for asking them, the ways in which they are posed and the thought processes that are necessary to produce an answer. The reasons for asking questions include:

- to establish levels of prior knowledge and understanding
- to check on the progress of learning and encourage further progress
- to encourage interest and engagement in the subject matter
- to stimulate curiosity and encourage motivation
- to access and implement cognitive 'thinking' skills
- to encourage debate, discussion and reasoned judgements.

The Ofsted inspection handbook (2012, updated April 2013) states that inspectors should see whether *'teachers use questioning and discussion to assess the effectiveness of their teaching and promote pupils' learning'*. There is a subtle difference here between assessment of pupil learning and a judgement, made by a reflective teacher, on how well he or she has promoted learning. This is a specific focus on how well a particular tool – questioning – has brought about a particular change – learning.

IRE model

IRE stands for the traditional Initiate–Response–Evaluate (IRE) model: teacher initiates question, pupil responds with answer, teacher comments on answer, often in quick-fire succession. IRE can be used to check on recall and factual knowledge, but is unlikely to lead to any real use of thought processes. The model is a closed loop when used in its traditional way. An example: 'Today we are learning about energy; John, what is energy measured in?' 'Joules, Sir'. 'Not just joules. Ben?' 'Kilojoules, Sir'. 'Correct, well done.' This I-R-E + I-R-E process has tested recall of knowledge, but not understanding (and even seems to have been 'bounced' in the class, when really it has just been repeated). The IRE process therefore needs to be expanded if it is to have any real value in a classroom.

Wait time

The quick-fire nature of IRE is one of its drawbacks. While it seems like progress is being made, more in-depth or well-thought-out answers are being snuffed out. One of the biggest issues for teachers is the effect of 'wait time'. Mary Rowe, in a number of studies, identified that teachers typically waited one second or less for a response, before moving on to another pupil or giving the answer themselves. She called this Wait Time 1. In addition, Rowe identified Wait Time 2, which is the pause time after a pupil response has been given. Her contention is that,

> If teachers can increase the average length of the pauses at both points, namely, after a question (wait time 1) and, even more important, after a student response (wait time 2) to 3 seconds or more, there are pronounced changes (usually regarded as improvements) in student use of language and logic as well as in student and teacher attitudes and expectations.
>
> (Rowe, 1986: 43)

It is therefore vital that you allow pupils time to think of responses and time to develop responses. Wait time 1 needs to be at least 3 seconds, possibly longer, a judgement that you will have to make depending on the age, level and subject that you are teaching. Wait time 2 could be even longer. This allows the pupil time to withdraw the answer and replace it with a better one or to expand or elaborate on the answer with further explanation or reasons for suggesting it. In the simple example above, a wait time 2 of a few seconds would have allowed John to go 'Joules, Sir,… no not just joules, kilojoules I think, because we need to measure them in thousands.'

PPPB

PPPB is a more recent suggestion that incorporates wait time 1. It stands for Pose, Pause, Pounce, Bounce. In this method, which is linked to formative assessment, the question is asked (Pose) and pupils think about the answer (Pause). Wait time 1 and 'no hands' will encourage reflective answers. A pupil is nominated to answer (Pounce). Make sure that your rules are understood – no help from others, no shouting out. Here you can use probing techniques (rephrasing, simplifying) to try to coax the answer out of the pupil if they are unable to respond immediately. Once you have a response, immediately open the question out (Bounce) to a second nominated pupil (is this right?, do you agree?, what can you add?). You can then open the question to the whole class. This method does not, of course, include wait time 2 or adequately explain the complex process of questioning.

Nine Ps

Nine Ps is suggested as a way to address the more complex elements of classroom questioning by including all of the parts needed for questioning to be effective. These are divided into three groups that loosely correspond to IRE.

- **Prepare.** Before a lesson you must decide not only what you are going to ask, but how and when (lesson opener, sequence of questions, consolidation of learning, plenary). You should also know which pupils to target with particular levels of questions. You should also have provided pupils with a context for the learning.

- **Pose.** Ask the question ensuring that you are using the right level of language so that all the pupils can understand.
- **Pause.** Allow wait time 1 for thought and reflection.

- **Pounce.** Nominate a pupil to answer the question.
- **Pause.** Allow wait time 2 for the pupil to develop his or her answer. If the answer is deemed inadequate or incomplete, then proceed to …
- **Probe.** Rephrase, simplify or break down into more accessible parts. If the latter, once the pupil has successfully answered a part, you can then probe further to coax more detailed answers.

- **Praise.** Congratulate the pupil on a correct answer – not too much, or it will smack of being patronising. Repeat the answer to acknowledge the pupil's contribution. Repeat it exactly as given; do not fall into the trap of 'tidying it up', otherwise it becomes your answer and not that of the pupil. If you want it clarified, ask the pupil or his or her peers to do so.
- **Peers.** There may be other possible answers and, particularly with higher-order questions, other opinions or judgements in the class. Repeating the response allows more thinking time for other pupils, and allows the question to be re-posed if necessary. For example: 'Andrew says wood has a lower carbon footprint than brick because wood eats carbon dioxide as it grows … is this quite right? What do you think, Ben?'
- **Persist.** If you find that you are getting little or no response, or the wrong response, persist with your line of questioning. Keep rephrasing, changing the language used or breaking the question down. Don't be tempted to answer the question yourself! You'd be surprised how often this happens, especially with trainee teachers, as the teacher is keen to 'move the lesson on' to a predetermined destination and extra time spent in encouraging responses is seen as wasted. It isn't.

Levels of questions

Questions can either be cognitive or non-cognitive. Non-cognitive questions require knowledge or recall of facts, without thought or analysis. Questions that work better are usually 'thinking' or cognitive questions for which there is no ready answer. Each can be lower or higher level, ranging from lower-level 'knowledge' through to higher-level 'analysis and evaluation'. Typically, at one end, lower-level non-cognitive questions ask pupils to identify, name, give, list or describe, whereas higher-level cognitive questions ask pupils to assess, decide, analyse, evaluate and make judgements, with reasons.

Closed questions

Lower-level questions are often 'closed', with the ultimate closed question being Boolean, i.e. where one response precludes the other. The most obvious of these is where the choice is between yes/no for the answer. Asking 'did you understand that?' is a Boolean question – the prompt is clearly that the pupil either did or didn't. What is more likely, of course, is that there is a grey area – some pupils understood some parts, some others, some most, some very little. But by limiting the response to 'yes' or 'no', all those shades of grey are eliminated. Closed questions do not have to be Boolean, but will have a very limited set of possible answers, which can be predicted by the teacher. It is therefore easier to get them 'right' but they require much less thought. An example of a closed question would be (in economics), 'what is inflation?'. This requires a definition, possibly a formula, but little else.

Other closed models involve the teacher providing prompts. This is sometimes called the '5 Ws' of Who, What, Where, When and Why. Three of these are closed, and useful to check knowledge. The very nature of the prompt Who, Where or When indicates a single word or short sentence answer. If, however, we add to these Why, How and What If (rather than What), this begins to prompt more open answers.

Open questions

Open questions are those with a variety of possible answers, often involving judgement or analysis. 'What If', in particular, requires pupils to bring in other information and predict, deduce or hypothesise. It therefore requires higher order skills of analysis and judgement. Open questions require the most wait time to realise their full potential. A particularly strong type of open question is to introduce controversy as a way of promoting discussion. For example: 'Well, of course all cosmetic treatments should be tested on animals, shouldn't they?' Open questions can also be set either before or as pupils enter the room in order to get them thinking.

Open questions are an important way of extending more able learners. In primary mathematics, instead of asking pupils to name a shape and identify the number or corners or sides simply say, '*tell me about this shape.*' One important question that all primary school teachers should ask in mathematics is '*how did you work it out?*' Children generate some superb strategies to arrive at an answer and sharing these increases the repertoire of available strategies for all pupils.

In literacy, *Community of Enquiry* encourages pupils to ask open questions. The class are introduced to a story. After hearing it being told, they are asked to sit in a circle and think of questions they wish to ask about the story. Their questions will be better if they have the chance to talk these through with a talk partner. This strategy is really effective when pupils are introduced to different versions of a traditional tale. It encourages them to think about whether the events are likely to be true and why a specific character behaved in a certain way. Try this approach with *The True Story of the Three Little Pigs!*

Key types of question

Some questions are 'specialist' enough to require a description of their own.

- **Canvass questions.** You may want a response from the whole class that is easy to see and to judge general progress. Responses need to be quick and visual, so for levels of understanding pupils can use, for example, thumbs up, down or across; traffic lights (red, amber, green Post-its® or cards); electronic voting buttons; ABCD cards; mini whiteboards or moving to specific parts of the room.
- **Scaffold questions.** This is a term given to the way you build progressive levels of difficulty into a question so that pupils are helped to build knowledge.
- **Consolidation questions.** A consolidation question will check that a concept or learning point is clearly understood. If it is not, this is your cue to switch back to scaffold questions. As the concept has already been taught, encourage explanations from the pupils. Wherever possible, do not tell them anything, but get them to tell you! Consolidation questions may arise through your facilitation. If you find yourself correcting the same misunderstanding, or facing the same reassurance questions, then this is the cue to pose the consolidation question. Wiliam (2011) refers to these as 'hinge' questions, pitched halfway through a lesson and requiring all pupils to respond within two minutes. Responses should be able to be collected quickly, so canvass response methods can be used.
- **Control questions.** Low-level, non-cognitive questions may be used as a technique to establish habits and good behaviour, or to reassert teacher control. For example, a post-plenary classroom leaving question session serves to give a quick check on learning and ensure engagement of all pupils. For example: all stand; pose questions (at the right level) for each pupil. A correct answer allows you to sit and be ready to leave (sometimes called an 'exit pass').

Pupils' questions

Pupils often ask reassurance questions to confirm that what they think is so, really is so. Straight confirmation will not assist the learning process, so use probes to check what is understood and encourage thinking to 'close the gaps' in understanding. Typically, showing work: 'Miss, have I got that right?' Your response: 'Do you think you have? Have you checked it against the example? What do your friends think?'

Pupils should be encouraged to ask searching questions at any point. To facilitate this, you can provide an anonymous box or ask pupils to write questions on Post-its®. These can be used to group questions by subject or difficulty. Pupils can then try to answer questions themselves, through recall, discussion or research.

Conclusion

There are several ways in which you can make your questioning less effective. These should be avoided and include:

- Choosing those who know the answer (i.e. hands-up).
- Repeating the pupil's answer but in your own words.
- Expanding on the answer way beyond what the pupil has said.
- Using correct answers as navigational beacons to guide you through your desired line of teaching – Black and Wiliam (1998) call this 'response seeking'.
- Sidelining the response. It is easy to praise, then reword and move on in the direction in which you had planned to move. Pupils could well perceive this as being ignored or patronised (well, you would, wouldn't you?).
- Language levels failing to adapt the language to suit the level of pupil understanding – too high, too difficult or low enough to be patronising.

Questioning should also provide data that informs teaching, so you need to keep a record of who you have asked and how. Techniques for this include building it into planning, making notes on a class list or tablet computer, random name generators, 'exit passes' and simple techniques like 'lolly sticks'. A set of lolly sticks containing names and basic data about pupils can be used to ensure all pupils are questioned at the right level and that all have answered. Choose a stick at random, ask the question and, if the answer is correct, store the stick; if incorrect, return it to the stack.

What we have learned

- That good questioning is key to good learning and progress
- That effective questioning is a key part of Ofsted judgements
- That there are different levels of question, with differing levels of effectiveness
- That there are different types of question, used for different reasons

Advice and ideas (1)

Provide the questions that you are going to pose in the next lesson as a 'thinking' homework. These should be open questions that require thought and reasoning but which serve to introduce the 'big issues' or key concepts that you intend to cover. While no written response is required, each pupil must be prepared to answer the question(s) posed. For example:

- In the book, who is the most interesting character? Why?
- In an ecosystem there are producers and consumers. What do you think this means? Why might it be important?
- Did England gain or lose from the Norman invasion? What evidence do you think you need to prove your point?

These are also called Rikki-Tikki-Tavi questions after the mongoose in Kipling's *Jungle Book* whose name means 'run and find out'!

Advice and ideas (2)

Black *et al*. (2002), having observed how 'hands up if you know the answer' worked in classrooms, suggested a technique called 'no hands'. If pupils are asked to raise their hands in response to a question, this tends to limit teacher interaction to that section of the class that knows the answer. If you impose 'no hands', this has the effect of involving everyone in the class, as anyone can be called on to answer. Even if the pupil you call on to respond does not know the answer, there are various techniques to encourage learning. For example, you can use positive signals, such as praise, to encourage an attempt to answer; you can probe further by rephrasing or simplifying the question; you can ask them to nominate a friend to answer on their behalf ('phone a friend'). This approach helps to focus pupil attention and involvement and, combined with wait time 1, will lead to better and more detailed answers.

What do you think . . .

... happens when you don't ask questions? In a history lesson, each group of pupils was given a set of resources and asked to form conclusions and write their own questions. The resources showed photographs of children working in mills, newspaper articles of the time by mill owners plus artefacts such as bobbins and cotton twine. Pupils were asked first to surmise what the pictures showed, then to devise their own questions regarding the resources using a pre-prepared sheet with the prompts who, what, where, when, why, how, what if. The questions were then exchanged with other groups and the answers shared table by table. Pupils therefore had to use their prior knowledge, their cognitive skills, their imagination and their analytical skills to make sense of the issue they were being asked to study.

Problem

Your questioning has become 'stale' and always seems to be either a general question on the whiteboard, or a straight verbal IRE with a pupil.

Solution

Jazz up the way that you ask questions by using games and quiz formats. Team or group competitions can be used, but try to make sure that it is the pupils generating the questions. Games include hot seating – the chosen pupil has to answer questions from peers; physically bouncing questions – pupils pose questions then throw a ball (or beanbag) to the pupil who must answer; weaving webs – pupils sit in a circle, pupil 1 has a ball of wool and, keeping hold of the end, throws it to a peer along with a question; the peer keeps hold of the wool and throws it to someone else creating a 'web' tracing the progress of the questioning. Any current TV quiz format can be adapted for the classroom with templates usually available online.

Recommended reading

Black, P., Harrison, C., Lee, C., Marshall, B.W. and Wiliam, D. (2002) *Working Inside the Black Box: Assessment for Learning in the Classroom*. London: King's College London.

Black, P. and Wiliam, D. (1998) Assessment and classroom learning, *Assessment in Education*, 5 (1): 7–74

Department for Education and Skills (DfES) (2004) *Strengthening Teaching and Learning in Science Using Different Pedagogies: Unit 1. Using Group Talk and Argument*. London: DfES.

Leven, T. and Long, R. (1981) *Effective Instruction*. Washington, DC: Association for Supervision and Curriculum Development.

Ofsted (2012) *School Inspection Handbook*. Available at: http://www.ofsted.gov.uk/resources/school-inspection-handbook-september-2012.

Rowe M.B. (1986) Wait time: slowing down may be a way of speeding up!, *Journal of Teacher Education*, 37: 43–50.

Wiliam, D. (2011) Raising educational achievement: why it matters, what has been tried, and why it hasn't worked. Presentation to the Ohio Innovative Learning Environments Conference. Available at: ileohio.org/materials/Documents/Wiliam_ILE2011.ppt.

Developing pupil learning skills

Links to Teachers' Standards

Standards Part One: Teaching
Standards Group 1: Set high expectations that inspire, motivate and challenge pupils

Introduction

Senior leaders in school and Ofsted inspectors are currently focusing sharply on pupils' learning rather than teaching in lessons. Lessons cannot be rated good or outstanding unless pupils' progress is also good or outstanding. Often during observations, beginning teachers focus too much on what they are doing rather than on what pupils are learning. You may have excellent presentational skills and be humorous and confident but, while these attributes are important, they are not as important as the quality of learning that is taking place.

To be good learners, your pupils need to understand what good learning looks like. Essentially, they need to know about the traits of a good learner. You cannot assume that your pupils will arrive in your lessons with the necessary skills to be good learners. Teaching is so much more than imparting knowledge to learners. Pupils need to take responsibility for their own learning and they need to under-stand their own role in accelerating their own progress. Making the skills of learning explicit to pupils will not guarantee effective learning but will go some way towards promoting it.

What does good learning look like?

As teachers we understand what it means to be a good learner. We have stud-ied hard, completed qualifications and achieved our aspirations. We have been good learners. Rightly we expect our pupils to be good learners and we get frus-trated when they become distracted, disruptive and give up easily. We expect that our pupils will value learning in the way we have valued learning throughout our school career and adult life. Despite our frustrations with our pupils, we really should not be too shocked. Many of our pupils may have been raised in families that do not value education. Some pupils are not exposed to good role models in the home. Additionally, there are social, emotional, cultural and linguistic factors that impact on learning. Pupils need to be supported in overcoming these barriers to enable them to make progress.

If we educate our pupils in what it means to be a good learner, they should gradu-ally be able to demonstrate these characteristics.

Building Learning Power

Building Learning Power is an approach developed by Guy Claxton and it has become popular in schools. Claxton (2002) identifies four key learning dispositions:

- **Resilience:** the learner's ability to persist with tasks even when they are chal-lenging.
- **Resourcefulness:** the learner's ability to use a variety of learning strategies.
- **Reflectiveness:** the learner's ability to evaluate their own learning and them-selves as a developing learner.
- **Reciprocity:** the ability to collaborate with others, to learn with and from others.

Building learning power encourages us to think of these dispositions as groups of *learning muscles*. We can develop our learning muscles to make them stronger. Each disposition is made up of a number of learning behaviours known as *capacities*. These are shown in the tables below (adapted from Gornall *et al.*, 2005):

Disposition: Resilience	Feeling (Emotional)
Absorption	Being immersed in learning
Managing distractions	Recognising distractions and walking away from them
Noticing	Careful observation
Perseverance	Persisting in the face of difficulties

Disposition: Resourcefulness	Thinking (Cognitive)
Questioning	Asking questions to yourself and others
Making links	Seeing connections
Imagining	Wondering *what if ...?* Using imagination
Reasoning	Working methodically Building arguments Explaining
Capitalising	Drawing together information from a range of sources

Disposition: Reflectiveness	Managing (Strategic)
Planning	Thinking ahead, planning what resources are needed and the time required
Revising	Willing to adapt in cases where things do not go according to plan
Distilling	Extracting essential features
Meta-learning	Knowing yourself as a learner and knowing how you learn best

Disposition: Reciprocity	Relating (Social)
Interdependence	Knowing when it is best to learn on your own or with others
Collaboration	Working together to solve problems Listening to other people's ideas Pulling on the strengths of teams
Empathy and listening	Really listening to others and understanding where they are coming from
Imitation	Adopting the habits that are observed in other people

This approach is most effective when it is embedded throughout the whole school, so that there is a consistent language of learning in all classes. When you observe pupils demonstrating the learning behaviours, they should be rewarded using positive descriptive praise: 'Lucy is doing some super collaboration; Tom is really persevering with that problem.'

You could display these learning dispositions in the classroom. It might be helpful to photograph pupils when they are displaying different learning behaviours. These photographs can subsequently be displayed and annotated to draw pupils' attention to the learning muscles that are being used.

Developing independence

One skill that teachers must facilitate in their pupils is the skill of being independent. There is little educational value in 'spoon-feeding' pupils. Ofsted will expect to see evidence of independent learning in classrooms. Pupils need to be taught how to find out information for themselves rather than simply being told it by the teacher. Developing independence in learning is a vital preparation for adult learning in further and higher education and within life itself. There won't always be a teacher around to supply the answers, so it is your duty to provide your learners with the necessary skills to make them independent learners.

Developing pupils' thinking skills

Anderson and Krathwohl (2001) revised Bloom's Taxonomy to be used to design learning activities that demand different order thinking skills. They suggest:

- **Low order thinking skills**
  - Remembering
  - Understanding
- **Middle order thinking skills**
  - Applying
- **Higher order thinking skills**
  - Analysing
  - Evaluating
  - Creating

The levels of cognition associated with each skill can be summarised as follows:

Skill	Cognition
Remembering *(low challenge)*	Recall of facts to answer a question Recall of knowledge to answer a question
Understanding	Processing knowledge to answer a question (for example, by explaining)
Applying	Using existing knowledge to solve new problems Applying prior knowledge to a new context

Skill	Cognition
Analysing	Breaking down what they know and reassembling it to solve a problem
Evaluating	Appraising something Defending something Formulating judgements Justifying opinions
Creating (high challenge)	Combining and selecting information from different sources to solve a problem

Make sure that the questions you ask (Chapter 8) and the tasks you set (Chapter 6) do not all result in low challenge. The taxonomy can be used to plan additional levels of challenge in tasks and questions to really stimulate pupils' thinking. You can also use the taxonomy to aid in differentiation. Possible questions to ask pupils using Anderson and Krathwohl's taxonomy are:

Skill	Possible questions
Remembering (low challenge)	What is the name of the dog in the story? How many sides has a triangle got? Where does the Queen live? What is the boiling point of water?
Understanding	Why did the wolf blow down the pigs' houses? Explain what evaporation means Outline the events that led to the First World War
Applying	Why do puddles dry up? Why do all the lights go out downstairs when one light goes out?
Analysing	What are the advantages and disadvantages of ...? Compare ... What would be the consequences of ...?
Evaluating	Was the wolf telling the truth in that story? Can you defend your position? Is this a valid argument? Why? Why not? How do you know that? What are the reasons? Can you give an example?
Creating (high challenge)	Can you give an alternative point of view? Can you design ...? Can you create ...? Can you compose ...? What would someone who disagreed with you say? Could you say that another way?

Planning tasks using Anderson and Krathwohl's taxonomy include:

Skill	Possible tasks
Remembering *(low challenge)*	**Matching games** Pupils match a series of technical terms to their definitions
Understanding	**Questions and answers?** Produce questions on different cards that require pupils to understand an aspect of learning and then produce answers on a set of different coloured cards. Ask pupils to match the questions to the answers.
Applying	**Find the answer** In pairs or small groups, give the pupils a key word. Ask them to create four to six questions. The answer to each question will be the given key word
Analysing	**Venn diagrams** Ask pupils to sort themes, topics or objects into different categories
Evaluating	**Diamond 9** Give pupils nine statements and ask them to arrange them into priorities from most important to least important by arranging them into the shape of a diamond
Creating *(high challenge)*	**Poster** After learning about a topic, ask the pupils to create a poster to synthesise the key information

Asking higher order questions

In your lessons, try to include a range of closed and open questions. Remember, closed questions require one response whereas open questions can elicit several responses. Examples of open questions include:

- Why do you think ...?
- What are some of the issues associated with ...?
- What would your advice be ...?
- What are the advantages/disadvantages of ...?
- How would you feel and why?
- What do you imagine?
- How is this similar to/different from ...?
- What do you believe?
- Is this fair? Why/Why not?

Understanding learning

To be good learners, pupils need to be able to understand the characteristics of effective learning. If they do not understand the learning dispositions which we expect them to demonstrate, they are instantly disadvantaged in the learning process. Effective teachers do not want their learners to sit in silence. They expect them to ask questions, to debate, to challenge or support the views of others, including those of the teacher, and to persist with their learning challenges when things get difficult. Good teachers do not spoon-feed their learners. They expect them to locate knowledge for themselves and to understand it. To reach higher levels of thinking, learners need to be able to apply their previous learning to new contexts and they should be able to analyse, evaluate and synthesise a range of information.

Conclusion

The ideas presented in this chapter have significant practical implications for the development of effective practice. Your pupils need to be able to understand what learning dispositions they are using and what skills they are demonstrating. If you make this explicit to pupils, then they are more likely to demonstrate these characteristics and skills more frequently.

Learning is not easy and at times it is challenging. As a teacher you need to take your pupils out of their comfort zones. If they never experience a challenge, it means that they are not learning on the edge of their *zone of proximal development* (Vygotsky). You also need to model being a learner. Great teachers are great learners and you should model the learning dispositions and skills that you are using explicitly to your learners. The best teachers keep learning but are also open to learning from their pupils. When this happens, you need to tell your pupils that they are great teachers because they have made you learn something new. Evidence of learning (progress) needs to be made visible in lessons but, just as important, the processes involved in learning also need to be made visible and explicit.

What we have learned

- Pupils need to know what good learning looks like so make the learning dispositions explicit
- Praise the pupils when they are demonstrating good learning dispositions and emphasise the dispositions they are using
- Celebrate good learning through displays of pupils demonstrating good learning dispositions and annotate these to draw attention to the dispositions that are being demonstrated
- Develop independence in learners – encourage them to find out information for themselves
- Reduce dependency on the teacher by teaching the pupils what to do when they are stuck

Advice and ideas (1)

The language of learning can be reinforced in different ways. The following ideas are adapted from Gornall et al. (2005):

The language of absorption	*You are really enjoying puzzling over that.* *You are really engaged/absorbed in that task.* *It feels good when you get right into an activity.*
Managing distractions	*What can you do to focus on what you need to do?* *Great! I noticed that you got back into your learning after that interruption.* *Imagine you are in a good place for learning. What is it like?*
Noticing	*You have noticed some important things.* *You have noticed a pattern.* *Look a little more. What else do you notice?* *Use your senses to help you notice.* *Can you see the difference between …?*
Perseverance	*How did it feel to persist with …?* *It's when you get stuck that you really begin to learn.* *Everyone finds learning difficult at times. See if you can persist a little longer.* *What do you need to do when you get stuck?* *Take a little break and come back to it later.*
Questioning	*That's a thoughtful question.* *That's a great question.* *What questions do you want to ask?* *It's okay not to know. What a brilliant question.*
Making links	*Can you see any connections?* *What do we know already that could help?* *Does this analogy help you to understand this?* *What else do you know?*
Imagining	*Try to picture … in your mind.* *Imagine what it would be like on the moon.* *What else do you imagine might be happening?* *You have used your imagination really well.* *Imagine what the world will look like in a thousand years from now.*
Reasoning	*That's a very good reason.* *Can you give a reason for that?* *What reasons can you give to support your answer?*
Capitalising	*How can we find out about that?* *What could help us with this?* *What skills do we need as a team to succeed in this task?* *Where could you find the information you need?* *Where could you look to find the answer?*

Planning	*What do you want to achieve?*
	What resources do you need to complete the task?
	How long do you think the task will take?
	What do you need to do first/next?
	That's a good plan! You have thought about lots of things.
Revising	*Good learners are flexible. They change things as they go along.*
	It is fine to change your plan as you go along.
	Learning doesn't always go according to plan. You can ditch your plan!
	There isn't just one way of doing things.
Distilling	*What are the three most important things in this text?*
	What are the bare bones of this?
	What is the essence of this?
	If you had to say one thing that you have learnt today, what would it be?
Meta-learning	*Which learning muscles work well for you?*
	Which learning muscles need more exercise?
	How do you learn best?
	Which way of learning worked best for you? Why?
Interdependence	*When is it good to learn by yourself?*
	Who do you learn with best?
	Do we need a group to be able to get that information?
	How does this help you to be a better learner?
	Maybe you need to go and think about this quietly by yourself for a while and then discuss it with others.
Collaboration	*How could you help each other?*
	That's good – you are finding it easier to work together.
	I noticed you working collaboratively.
	It is okay to ask other people for help.
Empathy and listening	*I saw you doing some really good listening.*
	Can you put yourself in X's shoes?
	How do you think X feels?
	Thank you for looking at me. That helps me to see that you are listening well.
Imitation	*Look carefully at someone who is doing it really well and see if you can do it like that.*
	Look at the way X is … [learning muscles]. Can you do that?

If your pupils are aware of these learning dispositions, they are more likely to demonstrate them.

What do you think . . .

… good learning means? What do pupils need to be able to demonstrate to show that they are being good learners?

Some pupils feel that their role as a learner is to sit quietly and listen to the teacher. However, is this good learning? Learners can easily be too passive in lessons and it is the role of the teacher to encourage pupils to actively participate in lessons and take responsibility for their own learning.

Problem

You may notice that pupils often do not persist with problems when they get stuck. They are often too dependent on the teacher and they will come to ask you rather than persevering with the task. You need to give your pupils some strategies to use if they get stuck.

Solution

Display a poster in your classroom entitled 'Some things to do if I get stuck'. Gornall *et al.* (2005) suggest the following strategies:

1. Ask a friend
2. Read the question again
3. Use a number line
4. Split the question up
5. Ask yourself – what do I know already that could help me?
6. Use a reference book
7. Use a dictionary
8. Use the Internet
9. Share the Internet
10. Go to another question and come back to the bit you are stuck on later.

Clearly not every strategy will apply to every situation but the general idea is to reduce reliance on the teacher.

Recommended reading

Anderson, L.W. and Krathwohl, D.R. (eds) (2001) *A Taxonomy for Learning, Teaching, and Assessing: A Revision of Bloom's Taxonomy of Educational Objectives.* New York: Longman.

Burnett, G. (2002) *Learning to Learn: Making Learning Work for All Students.* Carmarthen: Crown House Publishing.

Claxton, G. (2002) *Building Learning Power.* Bristol: TLO.

Gornall, S., Chambers, M.R. and Claxton, G. (2005) *Building Learning Power in Action.* Bristol: TLO.

CHAPTER 10

Assessment

Links to Teachers' Standards

Assessment underpins many of the Teachers' Standards
Standards Part One: Teaching
Standards Group 6 requires you to **make accurate and productive use of assessment.**
Without accurate assessment you will not be able to plan and teach well-structured
lessons (Group 4) or promote good progress and outcomes by pupils (Group 2). Assess-
ment should also lead to the identification of pupils' next steps in learning

Introduction

The current Ofsted inspection framework for schools emphasises pupil progress and your ability to secure progress over time. To do this effectively tasks must be pitched at the correct level for pupils to build on what they already know and can do. It is impossible to do this without accurate assessment. Tasks should be neither too easy nor too difficult, all learners should be challenged and new learning must take place within each lesson. Accurate assessment will help you to plan lessons that build on pupils' prior learning so that lesson time is not wasted on revising skills and knowledge that are already secure.

Assessment should be integral to your classroom practice rather than a 'bolt-on'. You will need to demonstrate that your lesson planning takes into account prior assessments of pupils' learning and to show that you are effectively using assessment both within and between lessons to advance pupils' progress. You will gradually begin to realise that you can only really learn about assessment through implementing it and using the outcomes to support your planning and teaching. It is critical that you recognise the link between assessment, planning and evaluation. Effective planning builds upon assessments of prior learning so that pupil progress can be accelerated. You will need to keep revisiting assessment throughout your career as a teacher through personal research and continuous professional development. It is a skill that many teachers find difficult but without it you will not be able to move pupils' learning forward.

Assessment for learning

Assessment for learning (AFL) or *formative assessment* has been defined as:

> … the process of seeking and interpreting evidence for use by learners and their teachers to decide where the learners are in their learning, where they need to go and how best to get there.
>
> (DCSF, 2008)

Research has found that this kind of assessment can enhance pupils' learning significantly (Black and Wiliam, 1998). The purpose of formative assessment is to inform learners of their next steps in learning and to provide them with advice on how these might be addressed. When conducted effectively, it provides information for teachers on what their learners need next. It should inform the planning process so that subsequent lessons and tasks that learners are presented with build on prior knowledge, skills and understanding.

Formative assessment is continuous. It should therefore be central to your classroom practice. It should take place minute by minute within lessons and at the end of lessons to inform subsequent planning for future learning. It is usually informal, and when it is used effectively it provides a powerful tool for accelerating pupils' progress. Formative assessment can take a variety of forms, including:

- questioning during lessons
- informal observations of pupils' learning
- capturing evidence of pupils' learning using photographs or digital footage
- feeding back to pupils about their work
- use of curricular targets
- self- and peer assessment
- reviewing and reflecting on learning with pupils.

This is not an exhaustive list but the purpose of these strategies is to enable you to understand what your pupils know and can do and to identify where they need to go next. The most effective teachers treat their pupils as partners in the process of learning. Involving your pupils in assessments of their progress helps to empower them. Involve pupils in reviewing their achievements and setting targets wherever possible because this will help them to become independent learners.

The aim of assessment *for* learning is to use assessment to promote learning. One of the underlying principles of formative assessment is to foster motivation so that learners feel empowered to address their targets. It is not a process by which pupils are graded or labelled into categories and it should always be sensitive and constructive so that pupils know what they have achieved but also know where they need to go next. Implicit within its principles is the assumption that all learners can continue to make further progress and it is your responsibility to ensure that they do.

Sharing learning objectives

Even the most experienced teacher can find it difficult to identify clear learning objectives for lessons. Your pupils need to know what they are learning in the lesson and they need to be able to articulate this. If they do not know what they are learning, they won't know whether they have learnt what they were supposed to learn. Additionally, if you are not clear about what your pupils are supposed to be learning, you will not be able to measure their progress during the lesson. Consequently, investing some time in thinking about the learning objective(s) will be time well spent because it will make assessment far easier.

Trainee teachers and even qualified teachers often struggle to differentiate between what pupils are *learning* in a lesson and what they are actually *doing*. You need to remember that the task that you provide them with is only a vehicle for enabling them to learn something (see Chapter 6). Remember, start with the intended learning and then design the task.

The National Curriculum is often the basis for identifying intended learning. The statutory programmes of study form the basis of what pupils must be taught. In the Early Years Foundation Stage, the Development Matters statements and the Early Learning Goals in the EYFS framework (DfE, 2012) provide the basis for what pupils need to learn. However, the statements of what pupils need to be taught in the curriculum frameworks are often too broad, vague and frequently not expressed in pupil-friendly terms. You may well need to break these down to make them more focused and you will almost certainly need to re-word them to make them accessible for your pupils. Remember, the statements are written for you rather than your pupils, but they still need to know what they are learning.

You need to make sure that you share the learning objective(s) with your pupils at the beginning of the lesson. It can be written on the board and it can be displayed on tables or in pupils' books. It needs to be embedded in the pupils' minds, so you could ask them to turn to their partner and tell them what they are learning. Alternatively, they could tell the wall, floor, ceiling, door or window! Keep it short and express it clearly in child-friendly language. Dissociate it from the context. If your pupils are learning to write a simple character profile from a character in a story, it is not necessary in the learning objective to identify the name of the specific character. If they are learning to write a recount of an educational visit, then the place name does not need to be identified in the learning objective. Once you have shared the learning objective with your pupils, keep reminding them throughout the lesson what they are learning. Do not allow them to forget what they are learning. Once everyone is really clear about what new learning should take place, it is possible to make an assessment of progress towards it at the end of the lesson.

Success criteria

Beginning teachers often struggle to identify success criteria. Criteria need to be expressed in simple pupil-friendly statements that can be displayed on the board, on tables or in pupils' books. They combine to enable the pupil to achieve the learning objective. Consider the following example.

Learning Objective: We are learning to write a recount.

Success Criteria:

- I can write an introduction, which includes details of time and place
- I can use four different time connectives
- I can write about four different events that happened during the day and put them in the correct order
- I can write a summary with an overall evaluation of the day.

The success criteria enable the pupils to see what success looks like. They can refer to them continuously throughout the lesson to assess their own work. Once they have achieved each criterion, they can tick it off. After learning has taken place or when a piece of work has been completed, the work should be assessed against the success criteria. Success criteria should be differentiated for different groups, so in the above example you could add in additional challenge for the pupils at a higher stage of development. In this instance, additional criteria might include:

- I can use four adjectives
- I can use four adverbs.

Consider how the criteria might be adapted for pupils at a lower stage of develop-ment. Process success criteria are particularly useful in some subjects and take pupils through the steps necessary to meet a specific learning objective. The steps could even be shown as rungs on a ladder.

Plenaries

The plenary should provide you with a valuable opportunity to assess the pupils' knowledge, skills and understanding gained during the lesson. It is an opportunity to make the progress visible. You could assess their understanding by asking them a range of questions. You could make this exciting by turning it into a game or a quiz (see Chapter 8). In addition, the plenary provides a valuable opportunity for pupils to assess other pupils' learning. You can display pupils' work for peer assessment against the success criteria using a visualiser or technology such as an iPad to photograph and project the work. This provides an opportunity for celebrating what has been done well and a chance for the pupils to identify targets for the child whose work is being displayed. You might want to use the acronyms **www** (what worked well) and **ebi** (even better if). The critical point is that you should always return to the success criteria in the plenary.

Self-assessment

Self-assessment is much easier if pupils have been given clear learning objectives and success criteria. Pupils should be encouraged to refer to the success criteria during the lesson to see if they have addressed all aspects. This can help them to make further progress. At the end of the lesson, pupils could be given an opportunity to assess their work/learning against the success criteria. Some schools use coloured pencils for pupils to indicate on their own work how well they think they have achieved the suc-cess criteria. This could be based on a traffic light model as follows:

Red = Success criteria not met
Amber = Success criteria partially met
Green = All success criteria met

You can also ask the pupils to refer to the success criteria to write a target. When you mark the work, you could add your own colour to indicate how well you think they have met the success criteria. In the plenary, you could ask children to position their names on a red, amber or green circle. This can be done manually using name cards but it can also be set up electronically using the interactive whiteboard. You can then store this as a record. However, if pupil self-assessments or your own assessments indicate that specific pupils have not fully met the success criteria, you will need to consider how you will provide additional intervention to enable these pupils to make further progress.

Peer assessment

Peer assessment provides learners with opportunities to provide each other with constructive feedback about learning. You need to train your pupils how to give sensitive and fair feedback, and you should establish clear consequences in cases where pupils fail to follow these principles. Peer assessment could take place at any point within a lesson but always uses the success criteria to identify successes and targets and to give advice on how to improve work.

Marking

The days of writing vague comments on pupils' work are well and truly over. Comments such as 'good work' or 'well done' are unhelpful because they fail to identify what the pupil has done well. Effective marking is not about awarding grades or marks out of ten. It is about identifying what aspects of the work are successful and stating developmental targets for future action.

Assessment of learning

Assessment of learning or *summative assessment* takes place at a fixed point in time. The purpose of summative assessment is to measure progress and attainment over time. It can take place at the end of a unit of work, the end of a year, the end of a Key Stage or at the end of formal education. It can be carried out using formal mechanisms such as tests and examinations or it can be based on continuous teacher assessment of pupils' learning over time. Schools have clear criteria for evaluating pupils' progress and attainment and you need to be familiar with these systems in every school in which you work.

Conclusion

Embedding formative assessment within your practice will enable you to plan lessons to meet the needs of the learners within your class. If your pupils are struggling to understand an aspect of learning, it is your responsibility to provide them with additional intervention to overcome their misconceptions. Frequent and accurate assessment will enable you to identify pupils' next steps and any gaps in their learning. Accurate matching of tasks to pupils' abilities and timely intervention with groups and individuals will help to accelerate pupil progress. Pupils should be viewed as partners in the process of assessment. Assessment is not something that should be done *to* them but rather it should be done *with* them. Giving pupils regular opportunities to reflect on their learning within lessons individually and with their peers and periodically with you will help them to understand their strengths and areas for development. Summative assessment serves broader purposes for schools, local authorities and the government. It provides information on how well the school is doing compared with other schools and whether value is being added to pupils. Summative assessment data can be used formatively to plan intervention to enable pupils to make further progress. If assessment is done properly, it does not limit what pupils are capable of achieving. Instead, it accelerates pupils' progress by clearly identifying future targets for learning.

What we have learned

- Assessment should inform subsequent lesson planning
- Assessment for learning is continuous and takes place within and between lessons
- Clear learning objectives and success criteria are essential if assessment is to be focused. This will aid self- and peer assessment.
- Pupils should be fully involved in assessment

Advice and ideas (1)

The key principles of effective marking/feedback are:

- Comments relate to how well pupils have met the success criteria.
- Praise should be specific: 'I like the way you have used different adjectives to describe nouns.'
- General comments about spelling, grammar and presentation should not be a focus unless these were stated in the success criteria.
- One target for action should be identified. This should be realistic so that pupils experience success.
- Consider giving the pupils a worked example to address the target in the feedback.
- Provide the pupils with further exercises to demonstrate that they have achieved the target.

Consider providing your pupils with response time to address the targets identified. This could be at the start of the day (in a primary school) or books could be given back to pupils before the next lesson (in a secondary school) so that pupils can act on the feedback.

Most schools now have strict marking policies, so you will need to be familiar with these. There may be a specific way of indicating successes in pupils' work and a specific way of stating targets. For example, many primary schools use 'two stars and a wish' to identify success and targets. Where possible, it is good practice to mark work with pupils in the lesson, and this is essential if you are working with younger pupils who require immediate feedback. Feedback for all pupils should be timely because it needs to be given while the lesson is still fresh in the pupils' minds. With very young pupils, feedback is often verbal and immediate.

Advice and ideas (2)

Mini-plenaries have almost become a buzzword in teaching. Exercise caution because if you over-use them within a lesson, you can stop children from learning and making progress. Essentially, a mini-plenary provides a useful tool for re-capping on learning during a lesson. You might stop the class to make a teaching point but they are most effective when your assessments within lessons indicate that pupils have misconceptions. Following your observations, you might use a mini-plenary to clarify a skill or a point. You might also want to use a mini-plenary just with one group of pupils to address a misconception. Furthermore, you might use a mini-plenary to accelerate progress further by introducing some new learning. This is most effective when learners appear to be easily grasping a task.

Consider using a mini-plenary to celebrate success. Visualisers and other technology can be used to present pupil work. Pupils benefit from seeing WAGOLLs (**W**hat a **G**ood **O**ne **L**ooks **L**ike). Seeing a good example helps other pupils to make better progress. However, too much teacher talk limits opportunities for pupils to learn, so try not to drop in a mini-plenary just for the sake of doing so!

Consider using 'Roam around the Room' instead of a traditional mini-plenary. At a given point, the teacher stops the pupils and asks them to 'Roam around the Room' as a magpie stealing good ideas from other pupils' work. Consider how you might use this in different subjects.

What do you think . . .

... about formal testing? The Statutory Assessment Tests at the end of the various Key Stages are high stakes for schools. Formative assessment provides useful information to pupils about their learning. Summative assessment often serves broader purposes in terms of schools being accountable to their stakeholders and notions of school effectiveness. Which form of assessment do you think is most important and why? How might summative assessment data be manipulated in ways that are detrimental to pupils' progress?

Problem

Parents often complain if teachers do not correct pupils' spelling, grammar and punctuation errors. This has resulted in some primary schools not sending home pupils' books at the end of the year.

Solution

Parents need to understand the school marking policy and the rationale which under-pins it. Schools can ensure that parents receive a copy of the policy. Some for-ward-thinking schools have even developed working parties of teachers, parents and pupils to formulate the policy jointly.

Recommended reading

Black, P.J. and Wiliam, D. (1988) Assessment and classroom learning, *Assessment in Education*, 5 (1): 7–74.

Department for Children, Schools and Families (DCSF) (2008) *The Assessment for Learning Strategy*. Nottingham: DCSF Publications.

Department for Education (DfE) (2012) *Statutory Framework for the Early Years Foundation Stage: Setting the Standards for Learning, Development and Care for Children from Birth to Five*. Available at: https://www.education.gov.uk/publications/standard/

CHAPTER

11

Using ICT to support your teaching

Links to Teachers' Standards

Standards Part One: Teaching
Standards Group 4: Plan and teach well-structured lessons

Introduction

Information and communications technology (ICT) has become a central feature of the classroom for all subjects, not just in its own right. Indeed, ICT as a subject will cease to exist from 2014, being replaced with computer science and information technology, and with a much greater emphasis on programming than hitherto. The uses of ICT have developed rapidly in recent years with the use of

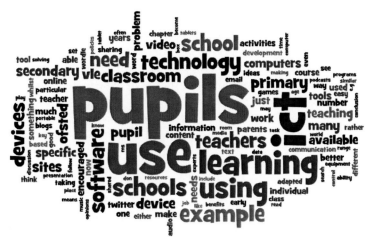

discussion groups, blogs, voting buttons, and so on being adopted alongside the more traditional areas of word processing, presentation software and email. Both computers themselves, and other technical equipment, have transformed classrooms and learning.

Computers have developed from the huge, slow, humming boxes with their green writing on a black screen to have more memory and computing power but also to be more adaptable, more flexible and, above all, more portable. They are easier to use and faster with a mobile smartphone now packing more hardware and software than a roomful of computers ten years ago. We now have a pocket-sized device that takes photographs and video, sends and receives email and texts, and on which you can watch films, TV and play games. Oh, and you can call people! Other technical equipment includes the ubiquitous presence of 'smart' interactive white-boards, of projection equipment, and of tools such as voting buttons and online polls. The challenge is to see how all of this technology can best be adapted for use in the classroom.

Using ICT sensibly

Your mission, as a beginning teacher, is to make sure that you know how to use the tools, and that you understand the sensible use of technology. The key word here is 'sensible'. The technology is a tool – just another instrument in your toolbox of ideas and activities. It is not something that 'must' be used just because it is available. Think of ICT as a hammer or screwdriver – if you have a particular job to do, choose the correct tool for the job. If it is not appropriate, then the tool stays in the box.

Benefits of using ICT

There are many benefits to using ICT. It can encourage creativity and innovation and help motivate learners. For example, pupils of lower ability are likely to write more. It can provide extra dimensions to learning such as images, audio and video that can bring the real world into the classroom. These are tools that have been available for a long time, but at much less convenience. Pictures had to be sourced and printed, video was available via tape or, later, DVD, but was still awkward to integrate into a lesson smoothly. The main benefit of such resources using ICT is that they are convenient. When an individual is using ICT, it automatically introduces an element of differentiation. Each pupil works at his or her own pace with a tool that is both patient and responsive. ICT can also be used for group and pair work and for sharing resources and outcomes. It also has the benefit of being non-judgemental and indifferent to distinctions of age, race, gender, religion, disability and ability.

The toolkit

The basic toolkit available in most computers is software for word processing, spreadsheets, databases, presentations and desktop publishing. While each does a specific job, most will multi-task – so, for example, a spreadsheet can double as a database. The Microsoft Office package is the most often available and the one on which many others are based. (In all cases, beware the default positions, as these will be American, e.g. American spelling and grammar.) In addition, there may be software to allow drawing, painting and music composition. Other programs tend to be specialist and perform specific tasks, such as early reading or storytelling programmes for primary children, or early years letter and object recognition.

Many standard programs are more powerful than either teachers or pupils realise. For example, Microsoft Word has an option that will check language levels so that, for example, pupils could be encouraged to rewrite work for a specific language level in English. In Microsoft Excel there is the scenario manager for 'what ifs' and the capacity to make multiple-choice questions using dropdown or interactive diagrams using sliders and scrollbars. The potential of Microsoft PowerPoint and similar presentation programs such as Apple's Keynote is hardly touched on by most pupils. What this does point up though, is that to be able to show pupils how to use ICT effectively, you need to know how to do so yourself.

Ofsted (2011) reported that teaching in primary schools was much better than that in secondary schools. Secondary schools were criticised for using a narrow range of vocational qualifications for ICT, not stretching able pupils, and not teaching control technology and data handling. In around two-thirds of primary schools, the teaching of ICT was good or outstanding. One of the Ofsted criticisms of ICT was that, particularly in secondary schools, teachers were only teaching with and encouraging pupils to use the software with which they were familiar and confident. It is outside the scope of this chapter to give specifics on these programs, but suffice it to say that a few sessions with your ICT experts in school will reap dividends.

Using tablet computers and smartphones

Portable devices now have similar power to desktop machines, and are considerably cheaper. The capacity of the device is important. It needs to do much more than just connect to the Internet or Intranet. It should also be able to edit text, and to upload and

edit photos, audio and video. Current thinking is moving in the direction of how their use can be integrated into the classroom, rather than banning them. Their use provides more choice and flexibility for solving a task or problem and allows for different ways to respond. Many built-in features can help promote learning. For example: translation software; recording audio and video (and uploading as podcasts or clips); using text (such as you sending text reminders to a class that a project or homework is due – easy to do and you don't have to reveal your phone number) and Twitter feeds. Other functions include sites where you can set up polling for free; wikis and blogs and specific tools like Wordle. Wordle provides a visual representation of text. On p. 93, for example, is a Wordle of the chapter. Here is a Wordle of a famous Shakespearean speech: how could you use it (or something like it)? Another idea could be to use QR codes embedded in tasks online or on paper – these could link to extra information or clues. This is a QR code that links to a site that creates QR codes.

Virtual learning environments

Virtual learning environments (VLE) are school-based online learning platforms that provide access to a range of tools. These include content, marking and assessment tools, classwork and homework activities, and lines of communication with pupils (and other staff). Teachers can, for example, receive work via the VLE (which can also check it for plagiarism), mark it and post feedback that can also be sent to a pupil's email account. In this way, handing in work on time is both encouraged and made convenient while fast, individual feedback is possible. Ofsted (2011) reported that most schools that they inspected in the period 2008–2011 either already had a VLE or were in the process of building one. They also stated that schools that made regular use of a VLE:

> … had been able to enhance and enrich many aspects of school life, including the quality of learning resources, communications with parents, and assessment and tracking processes.

Almost all schools now have some form of VLE, but their quality, use and development are hugely variable. In a number of cases, the VLE needs extremely careful management, as the lack of a search engine in some of them hobbles the user unless the content is set out with a crispness and clarity that makes it really easy to follow.

BYOD/BYOT?

Bring Your Own Device/Bring Your Own Technology (or even BYOP, Bring Your Own Phone) is an idea that has migrated from industry to education. In business, that an employee could use his or her own device was seen as an advantage to the company. Costs would be lower (especially capital costs) and employees would be more efficient. The downside was that company data could end up on a personal device and employees could, of course, choose to play games or email friends rather than work. The same issues arise in the classroom. Asking pupils to BYOD is a way of countering spending cuts, but also causes problems. While having the advantage of pupils using a device with which they are familiar, it has the disadvantage of being a device not accessible to the teacher. Detractors add that they feel that this is just a way to avoid the problem of constantly telling pupils to 'put your phone/tablet away' and making rules to banish them from the classroom and instead making the presence of such devices into a virtue.

There is also, of course, the question of equality of access and opportunity. How do you ensure that all pupils have the same or similar technology unless the school decides to issue them with devices? Schools also need to have policies in place to cover the use and misuse of own devices. These policies, signed up to by pupils and parents, are called AUPs or Acceptable Use Policies. Schools need the infrastructure of a decent broadband wifi system. Portals to the Internet can then be controlled quite effectively, but content contained on the device (and how it is shared between pupils) is not.

Whole-school mobile devices

Some schools have overcome the problem of BYOD by buying tablet computers for every pupil (BBC online, 2013). One Cornish school, for example, embarked on this course in 2011. Although there is an initial capital outlay (in its case, some £100,000 to equip 900 pupils), the aim is that the school can then dispense with textbooks and with what have become conventional devices. Equality was ensured by issuing each pupil with a device. Not only did teachers report better learning, but also pupils reported better teaching and parents were impressed. The school claims increases in achievement and that pupils are encouraged to read more widely.

Burden *et al.* (2012) evaluated a pilot scheme in Edinburgh, where tablet devices were provided to pupils in five primary and three secondary schools. There were four ways in which tablets were used: in class sets issued for specific use within the school; to individual pupils for use in all lessons but retained in the school; to individual pupils to use at school and at home; a combination of these, depending on age and task. The key findings showed that the higher the degree of personal ownership, the greater the benefits, in particular of pupils taking charge of their own learning. Achievement was improved, a 'wider range of learning activities' could be facilitated, and teachers were encouraged to use different learning activities – teachers were also issued with tablets and could develop learning activities on them, often in a collegiate fashion with colleagues. The research claims that:

Teachers have seen the emergence of a real learning community that extends beyond the academic to include a partnership between students and teachers who work closely together.

(Burden *et al.*, 2012: 10)

The conclusion has to be that, despite resistance, either school-provided tablets or BYO devices are the future.

ICT in the primary and early years classroom

The four themes of EYFS – the unique child, positive relationships, enabling environments, and learning and development – can all be underpinned by good practice in ICT. The ICT that pupils use has to be appropriate for their individual needs and stage of development. They need to be interested and stimulated by the ICT they are using, and to be able to learn through play, by exploring the nature and limitations of the technology in a safe environment. This learning can then be adapted so that it has a purpose. Positive relationships with ICT should be built between pupils in a class, so that they respect each other, and should also involve parents. Parents' knowledge and competence with ICT will vary widely, so take account of this in your planning. An enabling environment, in terms of ICT, means that technology should not only be available, but that children should be encouraged to use it. It should not be kept 'out of reach'. This has implications for safety and sharing, so needs to be clearly managed. Learning and development in ICT encompass moral issues of appropriateness, communication, problem solving and creativity. Visit the website http://ictearlyyears.e2bn.org/ for more details and ideas on how to plan and integrate good ICT in EYFS.

In addition, there are numerous different games and games sites that are either specifically designed to develop (for example) numeracy or literacy skills or problem solving or can be adapted to do so. Pupils should also be introduced to simple control from an early age. This includes programmable devices (such as video recorders), programmable music software, toys and specific devices such as 'Beebots'.

Conclusion

ICT as a support tool for learning is here to stay so, as a new teacher, you should be keen to make good use of it. This includes your own use of devices such as smartboards. It is easy to fall into the trap (identified by Ofsted) of only taking software as far as you need it to go to finish a particular task. Better to explore the software (and other technology) and see what its potential really is, then use this in your teaching. Of course, don't forget traditional skills that don't need ICT, such as creative writing, estimating, mental arithmetic and using hands to make and do things.

To many of us old lags it is amazing to think that the Web only recently (2013) celebrated its twentieth birthday. To pupils, however, it is something that has been there since they were born; they grew up with it and may be far more savvy about it than their teachers realise. What the Web has introduced us to is an easy way to search for and obtain information – probably in quantities that are much more than we actually need. This 'open door' also means that we can obtain incorrect or inaccurate information, pornography, scenes of violence and attempts at fraud. Access therefore needs to be managed, and pupils also need to be educated in what is and is not accurate. They need to be taught which are reliable sites and how to cross-check information. They also need to be taught how to search intelligently. Remember, child protection and online safety are still your responsibility, and these areas are covered in detail in Chapter 3.

What we have learned

- ICT has a key role to play in learning
- ICT must be used sensibly and appropriately
- The potential for ICT is often underestimated, so we need to explore what it can do
- Safety and safeguarding are central to ICT in schools

Advice and ideas (1)

What the online world has also given us are social networking sites and media that can be adapted for classroom use. Social networking media are essentially for sharing, so anything that needs or deserves to be shared can be, through various means. There are sites for sharing photographs, videos and written opinions, each of which has its own quirks. Used correctly, they can involve other members of staff, experts (around the globe) and pupils in the collaboration and communication. Some examples are:

- **Facebook:** pupils can create a Facebook page for a character from history, or from literature. Who were Hamlet's friends, what are his interests, how does he spend his time?
- **Wikis:** designed for webpage content to be added in collaboration with others. Wiki pages can be subject based, contain video, audio and links to other sites or podcasts.
- **Podcasts:** can be created by pupils adding to teacher-created content or to share learning. For example, an older pupil could be encouraged to consolidate learning by explaining a concept to a younger pupil, or to a parent.
- **Blogs:** pupils can follow blogposts (perhaps a scientist blogging an experiment, perhaps a sporting event in another language, e.g. the Tour de France in French) or create their own blogs for, say, learning 'journeys', problem solving or 'student voice' on an issue.

Advice and ideas (2)

Twitter is not just for letting the world know what you had for breakfast, or even for finding out what Stephen Fry is up to. There are a number of tools on Twitter that can be useful in the classroom. One of the main things it can do is to make something a shared experience. An English teacher could, for example, ask pupils to watch, say, a Jane Austen adaptation at home and set up a Twitter feed so that pupils can comment on it and their reactions to it. The conversation can then be continued in class and even used to create a webpage. You can use Twitter to contact experts in their field (such as NASA scientists), to generate, using Twitterfall, lists of Twitterfeeds containing a particular keyword (e.g. revolution, Jane Austen, inflation) to read discussions that are taking place. Geo-tagging can even show where they are taking place. You can also use the polling software (Twitterpolls) to collect pupil opinions or for pupils to collect opinions. By creating a hashtag for parents, they can also follow what pupils are doing and become involved.

What do you think . . .

... you can do to improve the use of ICT in your setting? Read the positive and negative aspects reported on by Ofsted and work out how you can build on the good and remove the bad.

Problem

You are timetabled for all your lessons in a computer room. This means you have to use the computers.

Solution

Many inexperienced teachers assume that because there are computers present, they have to use them. This is not the case, any more than it would be if you were timetabled into a laboratory or a gymnasium. There is often an element of pupil training required. Pupils may assume that, because they are in a computer room, the first thing they should do is to log on. Train them so that they only log on when you tell them to, and when there is something for them to do for which ICT is necessary. Remember, not everything has to be typed up – and it wouldn't be if what was sitting there were old-fashioned typewriters rather than computers!

Recommended reading

BBC online (2013) *Tablet School: Pupils Do Better at Mounts Bay Academy.* Available at: http://www.bbc.co.uk/news/uk-england-cornwall-22962670.

Burden, K., Hopkins, P., Male, T., Martin, S. and Trala, C. (2012) *iPad Scotland Evaluation.* University of Hull. Available at: http://www.ipadacademy.co.uk/wp-content/uploads/2012/12/Scotland-iPad-Evaluation.pdf.

Crawford, R. and McComish, J. (2012) Making sensible use of ICT, in N. Denby (ed.) *Training to Teach: A Guide for Students,* 2nd edn. London: Sage.

Ofsted (2011) *ICT in Schools 2008–11: An Evaluation of Information and Communication Technology Education in Schools in England.* Available at: www.ofsted.gov.uk/resources/110134.

CHAPTER

12

Delivering outstanding lessons

Links to Teachers' Standards

Standards Part One: Teaching
Standards Group 1: Set high expectations that inspire, motivate and challenge pupils

Introduction

An outstanding lesson is one in which teaching and learning are better than 'good'. Such lessons are one of the elements that go towards the setting of the overall inspection grade. Inspectors look for outstanding teaching and learning across the board in a school, so may make this judgement even if some lessons are not judged to be outstanding. Schools cannot be judged as 'outstanding' for overall effectiveness (i.e. cannot receive the 'headline' grade of 'outstanding') unless they have teaching that has been graded as 'outstanding'. Gaining such a judgement also helps a school to manage future inspections. Primary and secondary schools that are judged to be 'outstanding' overall are exempt from the normal cycle of inspections, which state that every school must be inspected within five school years from the end of the school year in which the last inspection took place.

Although an 'outstanding' school may be spared further inspections (unless it shows signs of deterioration), it may still 'be subject to inspection as part of a programme of surveys, of curriculum subjects and thematic reviews, including those focused on best practice' (Ofsted, 2013). Almost all schools, therefore, are subject to regular and almost notice-free inspection, making 'outstanding' teaching a goal that all wish to reach and maintain.

Ofsted

Ofsted is the acronym for the Office for Standards in Education. It has the responsibility to inspect education and to ensure that teaching and learning are taking place efficiently and effectively in a safe and healthy school atmosphere. Inspections cover every aspect of the provision and governance of a school, and the criteria that they are judging against are clearly laid down and available via the Ofsted website. In a typical inspection, a number of inspectors (depending on the size of the institution and the focus of the inspection) will give very little notice before descending on a school. The inspection will then follow a set framework and inspectors will report back their findings under set headings. Inspection reports are public property and all are published on the Ofsted website. A visit to www.ofsted.gov.uk/schools will provide clear information on the process and its possible outcomes. The framework for school inspection from September 2012 can be found at www.ofsted.gov.uk/resources.

These outcomes (which can lead to 'failing' schools being closed and 'outstanding' ones gaining increased funding or pupil numbers) are built from a number of areas, over some of which you will have little or no control. A key area, however, is that of teaching and learning in your own classroom. Although you may not like it, it is a fact of life that Ofsted will call in on your school in time. Inspections are, if anything, becoming more frequent, especially in order to ensure progress in schools that were deemed not to be making it.

Why watch me?

If you are a trainee, this could be as part of the inspection of your chosen training route, in which case the inspection will be focused not so much on you and your skills, but more on how the training provider and/or school and its systems are supporting you. For such provider inspections, it may be the mentoring, feedback or ITE provider support that is the focus, rather than the lesson.

Or you could just be inspected as part of the inspection of your school. Training teachers is a key role in schools, so there is no reason why you should feel that you might be exempt from such scrutiny just because you are a trainee. If this is the case, you should, of course, be judged as a trainee, rather than as a qualified teacher, but Ofsted no longer provides such guidelines, so be prepared to possibly be judged at a higher standard.

There is no reason why an inspector will specifically avoid a trainee teacher's lesson. Indeed, in some school inspections, the inspector may be investigating a particular line of enquiry (such as pupil behaviour, assessment policies or the delivery of phonics) and the trainee teacher's lesson may be the perfect place to witness this.

Inspections and observations are not supposed to be times of stress and terror, but are meant to be supportive and helpful – assisting trainees and schools to be better so that, in time, all will be graded as 'good or better'. However, you are likely to be at least vaguely panicked by the idea of someone coming in to pass judgement on you. You can help to minimise stress by knowing what it is that inspectors and observers are judging, and aiming to make these a part of your practice. If you are being observed by a mentor, or your provider tutor, you may still feel that you are under pressure but should remember that no-one watching you is making any sort of final judgement.

Trainee criteria

Training provider observers and mentors will have the sense to judge you against what they see as trainee criteria – they will judge you as a developing practitioner. It is worth knowing what the trainee characteristics were when Ofsted provided them in the 2008–11 Framework. No trainees were 'outstanding'; the designation at the top was 'very good', with the following features (Ofsted, 2011):

- Very good trainees have high and demanding expectations, based on thoughtful and thorough analysis of pupils' prior achievements. They are committed to raising achievement, and know how to accomplish this in ways appropriate to the pupils they are teaching. They play a full part in the life of the school and establish very productive relationships with pupils, teachers and other adults. They take the initiative, think rigorously and pursue their professional development across the life of the school. They set their current teaching within the wider framework of national trends and initiatives, to provide a context for its improvement.
- Very good trainees' knowledge and understanding of the subjects which they teach and of the broader education context in which they work are at a very high level. They use and apply their subject knowledge accurately and perceptively to consolidate and extend pupils' learning. They are confident and imaginative in their use of ICT, applying it productively to support their teaching and pupils' learning. They consistently enthuse and motivate pupils. They have an in-depth knowledge of the National Curriculum, National Strategies, and relevant guidance and statutory requirements and use them well to support planning, teaching and assessment. Their planning is consistently

of a very high standard; objectives, activities, resources and outcomes are all matched very well to the needs of the varying groups of pupils taught. A wide range of teaching strategies is used, with a good understanding of the particular contributions that different strategies make to pupils' gains in knowledge, understanding and skills. Evaluation of their teaching is rigorous and accurate and focuses specifically on what pupils have achieved in lessons. It is used effectively to improve their teaching.

- Very good trainees employ effective classroom management strategies and techniques for the range of classes they teach, which ensure that there is always a highly purposeful working atmosphere in which pupils learn at a substantial pace and enjoy what they do. They are adept and confident in using a range of assessment strategies, reflecting a clear understanding of the theory and practice of assessment. They are skilled at providing well-focused feedback and setting clear and precise targets for improvement. Their record-keeping is detailed, containing accurate and useful assessments of individuals as well as analyses of the performance of groups or whole classes. They use assessment information effectively to inform planning and teaching.

The Universities Council for the Education of Teachers (UCET), along with the National Association of School Based Teacher Trainers and the Higher Education Authority, have produced guidance as to how the 2012 Standards may be applied to trainee teachers. This may be found at www.UCET.ac.uk.

An outstanding lesson

So what is it that Ofsted is looking for? The first and key area that is judged is not just the teaching but how it is linked to the progress of the pupils. Does the teaching promote good learning? Is the learning evidenced in the progress that the pupils are making? Teachers are expected to know levels of pupil attainment and to expect and encourage progress. Such knowledge is not just gleaned from previous lessons, but by checking the progress of all pupils, in a systematic way, throughout the lesson – including making interventions as and when appropriate and by marking work regularly. Marking should provide appropriate praise, constructive comment and indicators for improvement (see Chapter 10). All such support and intervention should be individual, rather than general, and tailored to the particular pupil. This includes homework and other out-of-class tasks, which should be appropriate, integral and not just 'add-ons'. Inspectors also judge the atmosphere in which the teaching and learning take place, referring to this as the 'climate for learning'. In a positive climate for learning, pupils are interested and engaged, rather than demotivated (see Chapter 5).

Judging pupil progress

Ofsted judges lessons mainly on the progress of pupils within the lesson. The question that is posed is not 'was that good teaching?' but 'did good learning take place?'. Pupils do not have to be outstanding, or be making outstanding progress. What they do need to be doing is making progress within or beyond expectations. This means that you must be really clear on where they were at the start of the lesson, where they are at the end, and what evidence you have to support this. You must thus begin your planning by knowing exactly where the pupils sit on the achievement continuum – and where they ought to sit. Your starting point is thus previous assessments of pupil work, either by yourself or by other practitioners or agencies. Use pen portraits of pupils to note who is achieving what. Make sure that these are qualitative statements – that is, they should be statements about understanding and application, not just knowledge. That a pupil knows something is a starting point, but the knowledge is of no use until that pupil is able to apply that knowledge, relate it to a problem, analyse it and evaluate it. Armed with this knowledge, you can set tasks that are within the capabilities of the pupils. At the top end, pupils who have high levels of attainment should be stretched and encouraged to develop more of the higher-order learning skills. At the bottom end, pupils of lower attainment should be set tasks at a level where they can achieve. At all levels, tasks should be set so that pupils are not set up to fail, but also at a level where they must put in appropriate effort in order to succeed. Facing pupils with challenges that are too easy is just as counter-productive as facing them with tasks that are too hard. What you should be aiming for is 'baby bear' – neither too hot nor too cold, but 'just right'.

Planning to be outstanding

Knowing attainment levels is thus the crux of outstanding teaching and learning, from which all else follows. For example, resources (including other adults) are appropriate and efficiently used; work is varied and leads to progress in key skills such as communication, ICT, research and problem solving; homework is essential and integral. Progress is supported through appropriate questioning, assessment and adaptations to work and there is an obvious concern on the part of the teacher for the individual progress of each and every pupil. Pupils, faced with such meticulous planning and targeting, will be motivated and enthusiastic about learning.

There are a dozen key areas that are linked to this starting point, which may be bullet-pointed as follows:

- Resources, including teaching assistants where applicable, are highly effective in promoting rapid learning for groups of pupils regardless of their aptitudes and needs.
- Pupils with specific learning needs receive support at the time and level it is required to optimise their learning.
- The work includes opportunities to develop pupils' skills in reading, writing, mathematics and ICT, as well as providing opportunities for extending wider skills such as research and cooperative working.
- The tasks themselves enthuse pupils so that they persevere when faced with difficult problems and are keen to succeed and to learn more.
- There is no need for any overt discipline as pupils are engrossed in their work.

- The pace of learning will be optimised throughout the lesson if the teacher is able to use the time to the best effect in supporting pupils at the time they need such support.
- The teacher demonstrates a high degree of subject knowledge when framing and answering questions.
- Questions tease out pupils' understanding so that teachers are exceptionally aware of the degree to which pupils are secure.
- The work for each individual is adapted in the light of any misconceptions that are brought to light through questioning or checks on pupils' work.
- Marking is frequent and regular, providing pupils with very clear guidance on how work can be improved.
- The teacher ensures that corrections are carried out and any missing work is completed.
- Homework is an integral part of the lesson. It extends the learning and is treated as being as important as the lesson itself.

Conclusion

It is better to take a measured approach to improvement: to judge (or have others judge) where your strengths and weaknesses lie, and to plan lessons and activities to play to the strengths and address the weaknesses. Don't try to achieve all the areas that make up 'outstanding' in one go. Work on those areas that observations and your own reflections reveal to be weak. Planning an outstanding lesson for your mentor or tutor will put you in good stead for delivering an outstanding lesson for Ofsted or an interview. Start by knowing where pupils are on the attainment scale. All else follows from this.

The tasks and activities that you devise, the questions that you ask and the problems that you set can only be framed once this initial level of pupil attainment is known. You can then begin to judge how well you are achieving each outcome yourself, and consider how you can improve.

What we have learned

- Don't be scared by Ofsted, or other observers
- With sufficient planning, everyone is capable of being outstanding
- Start from the position of knowing the attainment of each pupil
- Judge where you think they can be challenged to be by the end of the lesson
- Set tasks that encourage them to reach this attainment, but which require effort to do so
- Monitor, assess and evaluate individual progress constantly
- Evaluate your own progress against the 'outstanding' criteria

What do you think . . .

... is the best way to keep the evidence that pupils are making progress? A book (or electronic device – tablet computer or portable device) with 'progress' written on it in big letters can be used and makes it obvious what you are doing. Recording progress should be overt, so that pupils get used to this and know if they are making progress and so you can intervene. Visit groups and individuals and, as part of your facilitation, ask questions and record understanding. If you ask 'can you explain why ...?' of a pupil and they can, then record this, share it with the pupil, and tell them the next target ('OK, so you know the main reasons for ..., now see if you can decide which are the more important ones and put them in order of priority').

AREA OF LESSON/ LESSON TIME or TITLE	Monday P4	Monday P5	Tuesday P1	Tuesday P5	Friday P3	TOTALS (Y)
Prior attainment levels						
Achievable work set						
Effective use of resources						
Support provided for pupils with specific learning needs						
Work in reading, writing, maths, ICT and wider skills such as problem solving and cooperation						
Tasks enthuse and interest the pupils						
No need for overt discipline, because pupils are interested and motivated						
Pace and timing are appropriately varied						
Subject knowledge is good						
Use of questions and questioning techniques						
Misconceptions were corrected						
Marking was frequent and regular						

AREA OF LESSON/ LESSON TIME or TITLE	Monday P4	Monday P5	Tuesday P1	Tuesday P5	Friday P3	TOTALS (Y)
I provided corrections and encouraged completion of work						
Homework was set and integral to the lesson						
Lesson judged as ...	X					

Advice and ideas (1)

Use the table above to judge both individual lessons and a series of lessons against 'outstanding' criteria. In each category were you Outstanding (3/3); Good (2/3); Satisfactory (1/3); Unsatisfactory (0/3)?

At **X** you can then see your own lesson judgement as follows:

- Outstanding (mostly outstanding with all at least good): 36–42
- Good with outstanding features (all at least good, some outstanding): 28–35
- Good (mostly good with all at least satisfactory): 22–28
- Satisfactory (mostly satisfactory): 11–21
- Unsatisfactory: 10 or under

You can also see in the Totals (Y) column which specific areas need working on over a series of lessons. For example, if 'homework' is rated at 15/15, then you've got it nailed; if its rated at 8 or below, you need to work on it and concentrate your efforts.

Advice and ideas (2)

Never devalue any of the skills that you have taught in a lesson by using them as a punishment. Setting a writing task as a punishment, for example, will only lead a pupil to consider writing in this negative light. For example, you may set a pupil to consider their behaviour by writing about it, but the action of writing in itself should not be the chore. Doing 'lines' (as Bart Simpson can testify) has never achieved anything. Think, also, about other teachers' lessons and the skills that they will have taught, before unwittingly undermining someone else's lesson by devaluing a skill essential to their subject.

Problem

In a history lesson, a large amount of effort had gone into preparation but the lesson was still not particularly effective. The teacher had a first-class degree in modern economic history but was trying to teach the Norman invasion. He played mediaeval music as the children entered; he had prepared cardboard weapons and he wore a paper crown on his head. He therefore knew that he had to engage, to promote interest and to encourage enquiry. The problem was in failing to make any explicit links between these items and the lesson content. They were therefore wasted.

Is it possible to learn to be outstanding when observations show that most teachers are not? Can we learn from poor teaching?

Solution

What tends to happen is that elements of a teacher's lesson will be good – and elements less than good. As an observer, what you should do is note the elements that are effective, and try to emulate them. So, what were the positive aspects of this lesson? At what points were the pupils engaged and interested? At what point did overt 'teaching' stop and learning take place? Perhaps the questioning was particularly good, or the idea of empathising with the soldiery. . . We should always look at the positives, and how to build on them.

Recommended reading

Glazzard, J. and Stokoe, J. (2011) Outstanding teaching, in *Achieving Outstanding on Your Teaching Placement: Early Years and Primary School-based Training*. London: Sage.

Ofsted (2011) *ICT in Schools 2008–11: An Evaluation of Information and Communication Technology Education in Schools in England*. Available at: www.ofsted.gov.uk/resources/110134.

Ofsted (2012) *School Inspection Handbook*. Available at: www.ofsted.gov.uk/resources/school-inspection-handbook-september-2012.

Ofsted (2013) *The Framework for School Inspection*. Available at: http://www.ofsted.gov.uk/resources/framework-for-school-inspection.

Pearson, J. (2012) Approaches to teaching and learning 2: planning, progression and sequence, in N. Denby (ed.) *Training to Teach: A Guide for Students*. London: Sage.

Your duties as a teacher

Links to Teachers' Standards

Standards Part One: Teaching
Standards Group 8: Fulfil wider professional responsibilities
Standards Part Two addresses your professional duties as a teacher

Introduction

Fundamentally, your key duty aside from safeguarding the safety and wellbeing of pupils in your care is to ensure good pupil progress. This is predicated on good subject knowledge, good assessment and clear planning. However, you also have a responsibility to build effective relationships with other colleagues, pupils, parents and carers. You must conduct yourself in a professional manner both inside and outside school and you must ensure that you comply with the various codes of professional conduct that apply to you.

Teaching is a profession and from the moment you begin to train as a teacher, you should view yourself as a professional. Part Two of the Teachers' Standards outlines the professional duties of all teachers. However, all training providers and most schools now set out their own codes of professional conduct that are more detailed than the Teachers' Standards. Your training provider, parents, colleagues and pupils will expect you to conduct yourself in a professional manner at all times.

Conduct

Your conduct out of school must not bring the school into disrepute. Set up stringent privacy settings on your private social network accounts so that your account cannot be accessed by pupils or parents. Carefully consider where you choose to socialise. It may also be easier for you to live outside of the school catchment area. Parents and pupils always view you as a teacher even if they see you outside of school, so they will not expect to see you behaving in a manner that is unprofessional and inconsistent with their view of teachers.

There is an expectation that you will treat all people with respect and dignity, including demonstrating respect for people of different faiths. Your personal views must not undermine fundamental British values of tolerance and respect for the rights of others. Demonstrate positive attitudes towards all people, including those from minority groups. If your own personal values clash with this, then it is your responsibility to keep these in check.

Absence

Absent teachers have a detrimental impact on pupils' progress. If you are absent from school, your classes will need to be covered by agency staff, other teachers in school or cover supervisors. Although many are excellent, pupils will inevitably test the boundaries with new staff, resulting in loss of learning time. Being absent from school increases the pressure on colleagues who may be pulled away from their usual duties to cover your classes. Being absent from school is thus not a decision that you should make lightly. Think seriously about the consequences in terms of your pupils and your reputation before you take time off. That said, if you are too ill to teach, you will have no choice but to be absent. There will be procedures in the school's code of conduct for reporting absence and your training provider will also have a clear policy on this. There may also be an expectation that you provide lesson plans so that colleagues can pick up from where you left off.

Punctuality

Poor punctuality is inexcusable in most jobs and teaching is no exception. Training providers will stipulate a time when teachers need to be in attendance. Schools will each have different daily structures. There will be lessons and resources to prepare and you may be required to attend a staff briefing before teaching starts. Try to get as much preparation done the night before so that you are more organised in the morning. You need to feel calm when your pupils arrive into lessons, so try to pace yourself from the point when you arrive in school to when lessons start.

Safeguarding

Your responsibility to safeguard the welfare of your pupils and your duties in relation to safeguarding are explained in Chapter 3. It is your responsibility to familiarise yourself with the safeguarding policy and to ensure that any concerns about specific children or pupil disclosures of abuse are passed on to the nominated safeguarding officer. If you are planning lessons that involve an element of risk, you will need to ensure that you have completed the appropriate risk assessments and that there is a written record of this. If you are planning an educational visit, the necessary risk assessment and documentation associated with the visit must be completed and approved by the governors and local authority before the visit takes place. Talk to the nominated person for educational visits and ask him or her to go through the procedures with you.

Contributing to the life and ethos of the school

Each school has its own ethos, which is the guiding beliefs or ideals that make it distinct and characterise it. When you apply for a teaching post you will get a feel for the ethos when you walk around the school. The ethos may also be communicated in various ways, for example, through displays, or it may be written into the school prospectus, policy documentation and communicated via the school website. Before you apply for a teaching post you need to ensure that you can fully support the ethos of the school. The ethos should have been formulated collectively through extensive collaboration with staff, pupils and parents, thus you are not in a position to change it as an individual.

Take time to read the school's policies, as you will be expected to comply with them. Again, the policies should have been formulated after extensive collaboration with pupils, parents and colleagues. Ofsted inspectors will monitor that school policies are being implemented in practice. Check that you are following the agreed school marking policy and implementing the agreed systems for managing pupil behaviour. Schools may also have policies about staff dress or the teaching and learning environment. The aim of policies is to ensure that there is consistency across the school, which ensures that pupils receive similar messages from class to class or teacher to teacher.

Be a team member

As a beginning teacher you will inevitably focus initially on your own teaching and teaching base. However, you must remember that you are working as part of a team, so it is important that you do not isolate yourself. Talk to your colleagues and visit other classrooms to 'magpie' the best ideas for your own practice. There will be certain tasks at specific times during the year that need to be done collectively and you need to play your part in working as a member of a team.

Involve yourself fully in the wider life of the school, for example, through after-school clubs, school productions and school fairs. Schools are social places and pupils' holistic development is important to enable them to be fully rounded members of society. Schools are also part of their communities rather than distinct, so take every opportunity to support community events.

Developing relationships with mentors

As a beginning teacher it is important that you develop a good working relationship with your mentor. At this stage of your development, they will not expect you to know all there is to know about teaching. Indeed, one of the joys of teaching is that teachers never stop learning because education is constantly changing and learners keep presenting different challenges.

Work with your mentor to identify some initial targets for your development. Ensure that these are SMART targets (specific, measurable, attainable, realistic and timed). Try to avoid vague targets such as to 'develop my knowledge of assessment' or 'develop my behaviour management skills'. Targets need to be specific. Which aspects of assessment or behaviour management, for example? Maybe how to implement the marking policy or develop pupil self- or peer assessment. Or maybe the use of positive, descriptive praise or non-verbal strategies. Keep the targets focused and really sharp. Keep a log of how you have addressed the targets, so that you are able to demonstrate that you have made progress.

Your mentor will expect you to ask questions. Do not pretend that you know everything at this stage of your development. Initially, you may need some support with planning or aspects of classroom organisation and it is perfectly acceptable to go to your mentor (or indeed other colleagues) to ask for advice. It shows that you are willing to learn from other people's experience. As you gain more experience, you will require less support.

Alongside formal observations of your teaching, it is perfectly acceptable to ask your mentor or other colleagues to carry out informal observations to aid your development. In primary schools you can draw upon the advice of subject leaders for specific subject advice.

Relationships with colleagues

Learning to manage conflict with colleagues is important because inevitably you will experience some conflict working in schools. Teaching is a demanding and exhausting profession and as the term or year progresses, people can become more irritable. If a colleague has upset you, the best way of dealing with this is to talk it through with them. It is not advisable to talk to other people or the senior leadership team before you have addressed your concerns to the colleague that they relate to. Keep calm and remain professional at all times. Listen to his or her point of view and agree a way forward. Ultimately, you have to work together and there is no point in bearing grudges. If you have done something to upset a colleague, be prepared to apologise and move on!

Get to know the clerical and ancillary staff. Schools cannot function without all the cogs and therefore all parts of the machinery of a school serve an important purpose. Do not assume that you are more important than other colleagues. Building a relationship with these colleagues is key because if they like you, they will go out of their way to help you. Ensure that your pupils take responsibility for leaving the classroom tidy at the end of the day so that the cleaners can do their jobs. Cleaners are not paid to pick up pencils! Negotiate with the appropriate ancillary staff if you need to come into school during holidays or to stay late after school.

Working with multi-agency teams

As a beginning teacher you may find that multi-agency teams are supporting some of your pupils. These could include:

- educational psychologists
- speech and language therapists
- occupational therapists
- physiotherapists
- behaviour support workers
- nurses
- social workers
- learning support teachers from the local authority.

This is not an exhaustive list. One significant challenge will be finding the time to meet with these colleagues to discuss a particular child. Their roles vary from supporting the pupil within lessons, observing the pupil in class, carrying out assessments and implementing interventions. Quickly establish professional and positive working relationships with these experts and be prepared to implement any advice that they provide. You will be expected to meet with these professionals periodically to review the strategies, and parents and carers should be included in this process.

Effectively deploying support staff

Developing effective working relationships with support staff is vital if you are to maximise outcomes for pupils. Demonstrate that you value the contribution that they can make to supporting learning and plan for their effective deployment in lessons. Their roles vary from being assigned to support an individual pupil to supporting small groups of pupils. Support staff should have a striking impact on supporting pupils' learning. Gone are the days when they spent their time mounting work and putting up displays!

You must find time to communicate sufficiently with them before the start of lessons. This can be challenging, especially if staff are not contracted to begin work until 9 am.

Provide support staff with a concise briefing sheet that outlines the intended learning and the tasks to be undertaken. Include space for them to record assessments of specific pupils, as this information can then inform your subsequent planning. Try to involve support staff in the planning process, even if this is only done verbally. During any teacher exposition phases, ask them to be active, rather than just listen to you. For example, they can support individual pupils who need the content breaking down further or sit next to specific pupils to help with the management of their behaviour. You might ask them to make observational assessments of specific pupils or they could team teach with you. The point is that they need to be deployed in supporting learning rather than washing paint pots or setting out resources.

Remember that support staff could be deployed to support more able as well as less able learners. This is an important point because often they are assigned to less able groups but you also have to take responsibility for educating these groups. Deploying your support staff to support more able pupils will allow you to work with pupils at lower stages of their development. Wherever possible ensure that they support individual pupils within a group situation. The one-to-one model often promotes a culture of dependency and limits interaction between some pupils and their peers. This is essential to promote learning because pupils learn from each other.

During the plenary, support staff could provide additional intervention for specific individuals who have struggled in the lesson or they could team teach with you. Again, their time should not be wasted by listening to you.

Managing your professional development

Beginning teachers are expected to manage their own professional development time. This is allocated as non-teaching time to develop knowledge, skills and understanding about teaching. It is not an extension of your planning, preparation and assessment (PPA) time. You could use this time to:

- observe good and outstanding teachers in your school and in other schools
- visit other schools to develop your own knowledge
- work with your mentor
- attend teacher professional development courses.

Professional development activities must be aligned to the targets that you have identified with your mentor. If you need to, work on an aspect of behaviour management; for example, observe teachers who demonstrate excellent behaviour management skills. If you choose to visit another school, make sure that there is a clear focus to the visit; for example, you might want to observe how assessment for learning is embedded. Make sure that you disseminate anything that is worthwhile to your colleagues back in your own school. Keep a record of your professional development activities and its impact on your own pupils so that senior leaders can evaluate its impact.

Developing partnerships with parents and carers

Parents are partners in pupils' learning and you should aim to develop effective, professional relationships with them. Parents are also key stakeholders in education and Ofsted inspections focus on how well schools work in partnership with parents to raise outcomes for pupils. Listen to the concerns of parents and carers and take them seriously by demonstrating how you will address these. Establish open relationships so that parents feel able to approach you and make suggestions to improve your practice. Often parents have brilliant ideas that teachers have not even considered.

Working in partnership with your pupils

Your pupils are entitled to a say about their education. Their voices should be listened to and acted upon. Try to develop professional but caring relationships with your pupils. Demonstrate that you value them as people and that you value their ideas. Give them opportunities to express their views about their lessons and allow them to shape their own learning experiences. Pupils can take some responsibility for the identification of lesson content. Providing pupils with regular opportunities to give feedback about their education is an important way of maintaining effective pupil–teacher relationships and empowering pupils to effect change. Involve your pupils in assessing their own learning and setting targets for their own learning and behaviour.

Conclusion

You must ensure that your pupils make good progress and this is unlikely to be secured without good subject knowledge, assessment, planning and behaviour management. All the groups of standards therefore combine to ensure that pupils are making good progress and securing good outcomes. As a teacher you do not have to do all of this in isolation. You will work in collaboration with support staff, external agencies, pupils, and parents and carers to secure good progress. It is your responsibility to develop good working relationships with all of these people to maximise outcomes for your pupils.

What we have learned

- You must be professional at all times
- Be sure that you are able to support the school's ethos before you accept a teaching position
- It is important to develop effective working relationships with all colleagues in school
- Parents, carers and pupils are partners and should be treated as such

Advice and ideas (1)

To someone from an office or factory environment, school days appear very short. This is because time is used for preparation, marking and other duties outside the core teaching hours. If you treat the school day as finishing at 5 pm, for instance, this gives you between one and two hours of working time. Usually you can stay on the school premises for this time. This means that when you do get home, you can relax!

Advice and ideas (2)

Parents' consultation meetings can cause beginning teachers some anxiety. You can never really be sure what parents think about you or what they might say to you but you only have a short time to get your points across. Always try to say something positive about their child and don't communicate too many targets for their child's development. Always be honest with them. There is little point in telling them their child is a genius when everyone knows that they are not! Give them an indication of what level their child has reached and their targets. Make suggestions in terms of how they might help their child to reach these targets and end with something positive and a smile. Do not focus exclusively on the pupil's performance in various subjects. Make sure that you acknowledge other attributes that their child is able to demonstrate, for example, friendliness, perseverance, kindness, and so on. Ultimately, most parents want to know if their child is happy in school, so do not underplay the non-academic aspects which parents may value.

What do you think . . .

... would be revealed if a pupil accessed your Facebook page? What steps should you therefore take to ensure this doesn't happen?

Problem

How would you deal with an irate parent coming into school one morning?

Solution

If the parent is aggressive, ask them to leave immediately and inform them that you will happily speak to them when they are calm. Make sure they are moved away from any pupils. Ask them to make an appointment to discuss the issue at lunchtime or at the end of the day but do not see them immediately. This will buy you thinking time and give you an opportunity to reflect on how you will address the parent's concerns. If you are anxious about the meeting, ask a more experienced colleague to sit in for moral support. Ask the parent to sit down so that you are both on the same level and open the discussion by giving them time to talk through concerns. Listen to them, nod and make the odd note but try not to interrupt them. Let them get it off their chest. Then offer a response but acknowledge that you understand why they might be upset. Agree a resolution by stating what action will be taken to address the issue. Make a note of this so that the parent can see that you have taken their concerns seriously. Then make sure that you follow this up.

Recommended reading

Denby, N. (ed.) (2012) *Training to Teach: A Guide for Students*. London: Sage.

CHAPTER 14

Managing a workload

Links to Teachers' Standards

Standards Part One: Teaching
Standards Group 2: Managing your workload effectively will help to ensure that you promote good progress and outcomes by pupils

Introduction

You will find that your training is incredibly demanding and there will be competing priorities which you will be expected to fulfil. During your training, you will complete blocks of time in school in order to help you master the skills associated with teaching. These include writing assignments, planning lessons and sequences of lessons, evaluating your teaching and keeping up to date with assessments, record keeping and marking. It is important to establish a work–life balance and develop a clear separation of home and school.

Teaching is a vocation

Inevitably you will look forward to starting your teaching career and you may have been told that life will become easier when you qualify. The reality is that this will not be the case, particularly if you want to make a good impression and perform to a consistently good standard. Good teachers invest a great deal of time in their careers. For these teachers, teaching is something which they are interested in, passionate about and it is more than a job. It is a vocation. Good or outstanding teachers work hard and often in excess of their directed time. In general, teachers are committed, dedicated professionals despite the messages that are conveyed in the press and irrespective of their perceived teaching ability.

Expectations

The roles and responsibilities of a teacher usually cannot be undertaken within school working hours because of the tasks that it is necessary to complete. You will need to be prepared to work in the evenings, at weekends and during school holidays. The holidays are for the pupils and there is an unwritten expectation that you will work during at least some of these. You cannot expect to have credibility among your colleagues and parents if you put in the minimum amount of time and spend every school holiday on a foreign beach! Teachers have been granted some time within their timetables for planning, preparation and assessment. It is unlikely that you will be able to do all that you need to do in this time and you should be prepared to take work home with you.

During your initial training you will spend a great deal of time planning your lessons in detail. This is necessary because you are new to teaching and you do not have the experience needed to take short cuts. The lesson plan will help you to mentally rehearse the lesson before you teach it. This will give you a sense of confidence because you should know what you are doing. Once you qualify as a teacher, you should not need to plan your lessons in as much detail and you might well be able to work from medium-term plans or weekly plans. You will need to follow the expectations of your school's leadership team and many head teachers request that planning is uploaded onto a shared drive on a weekly basis. Remember, however, you are still training in your first year of teaching (and still learning every year afterwards). Also, you will have many more responsibilities to undertake as a serving teacher than as a trainee. Teaching for real is not easier than training to teach, it is just different.

Challenges

So what are the challenges that you will face? Lessons will need to be planned and resources will need to be prepared and sourced. You will be expected to keep up to date with your pupil assessments and record keeping and you will be expected to mark pupils' work in a timely fashion. Homework will need to be set and marked. You will be required to write individual education plans or behaviour plans for pupils with additional needs and these will need to be evaluated and updated on a regular basis throughout the year. You will be required to attend meetings with your leadership team, colleagues from other agencies and parents to discuss pupils' progress. You will be expected to write written reports on every pupil in your class and attend parent consultation meetings at least twice a year.

Then there are the meetings! As a class teacher or subject teacher you will need to meet regularly with your immediate line manager(s) to discuss priorities and to evaluate progress. You are contractually obliged to attend staff meetings after school and you may be required to attend meetings to give you an opportunity to share practice with teachers in other schools. You will be required to attend courses of continuing professional development, many of which take place in the evening. As you gain experience you may choose to become a member of the school governing body. There are many meetings to attend and these often carry on well into the evening. You will need to allocate time to analyse pupil performance data for the classes that you teach and identify any pupils who need additional intervention and even extra-curricular classes. You might also be required to attend school and community events in the evening, at weekend or during the holidays.

No one term is less demanding than another in teaching. The pressure is on teachers and pupils constantly. This is partly because pupils are now assessed frequently during the year and teachers need to be able to demonstrate that their pupils are making consistently good progress. You cannot afford to wait until the end of the academic year to discover that a pupil has not made adequate progress. You need to be constantly tracking pupil progress and intervening in a timely manner to accelerate their progress. Additionally, as a teacher you will be observed regularly and your pupil progress data will be scrutinised by your leadership team on a very regular basis. This is one way of monitoring the quality of your teaching from a distance.

Housekeeping

You will need to keep your classroom environment looking good. This includes setting up the classroom in the first place, putting up displays and labelling resources. There will be a plethora of administrative duties that you will be required to undertake. These include filling in behaviour logs, writing risk assessments, producing letters for parents and organising educational visits. As a teacher you do not have the luxury of your own personal assistant! You may well have to do your own photocopying and laminating, so you need to be prepared for this. This list is not exhaustive.

Leadership

As you gain further experience you may be asked to take on subject leadership responsibility or you may choose to move into senior leadership roles. Leadership brings with it enormous challenges. As a leader with a teaching responsibility you will want to do both roles well. You will not want your teaching to slip but great demands will be made on your time in relation to fulfilling your leadership role. You may be required to quality assure the teaching within your subject across the school. This means observing lessons, writing feedback reports and giving oral feedback to colleagues. You will write action plans for your subject or area and these will need to be regularly reviewed. You will be required to analyse pupil performance data within your subject and you will be expected to hold your colleagues to account in cases where pupils are not making good progress. You will need to contribute to the school self-evaluation form (SEF) and the school development plan (SDP). You may be asked to support less experienced or weaker teachers or trainees through coaching and mentoring programmes. As you undertake all of these tasks, you will need to be extremely efficient in order to balance these responsibilities with your teaching commitments. As a leader your teaching will need to be at least consistently good but you will also need to ensure that you are carrying out your wider responsibilities.

Work–life balance

Inevitably, all of these tasks cannot be completed within school hours and you will need to decide how much time you are prepared to spend out of school on fulfilling your professional responsibilities. You will also need to preserve some time for yourself because to be effective in school you need to be refreshed and energised. Make the most of your available time in school. Try not to waste too much time socialising with colleagues because inevitably you will pay the price for this by having to take work home with you. Although it is important to socialise and establish relationships with colleagues, it is also important to complete the tasks that you need to do. Try to work efficiently and use your planning, preparation and assessment time wisely. Allocate specific amounts of time for specific tasks. If you need to mark three essays in one hour, do try very hard to stick to this. Allocate specific time periods for your planning and assessment and work within these limits. You may well be a perfectionist but you will soon realise in teaching that you need to cut corners to get everything done on time. Do not spend an hour doing a job that can be completed in ten minutes. Allocate windows of time for specific jobs.

Highly committed teachers find it difficult to establish a work–life balance. Some teachers spend all their personal time on their schoolwork and are unable to stop thinking about school. However, establishing a clear division between home and school is important because developing a work–life balance will inevitably reduce your stress and anxiety. You will feel more refreshed in work if you have spent some time doing other things. If you do not establish a work–life balance, you risk 'burn-out', and this could result in you being very ill and needing to take time off.

Sharing resources

Try hard to find short cuts. As a teacher there is no need for you to reinvent the wheel! If someone has a resource that you can use, there is no point wasting time producing that same resource yourself. Share resources with your colleagues and let them share their resources with you. Do not waste time making resources that can only be used once. This is not an efficient use of your time. When you plan lessons, consider from the outset how much preparation will be required to resource the lesson. It is inefficient to spend twelve hours planning a one-hour lesson! Is that presentation really necessary if it takes six hours to produce? Discuss your planning with your colleagues. They may be able to help you resource the lesson. In an ideal world, all teachers would present their pupils with high-quality, attractive resources. However, in the real world of teaching this is unrealistic. Some of the best lessons may well require hardly any resources because you are the most important resource to your pupils.

Using support staff

Develop effective relationships with your support staff. They may be able to complete some of the tasks for you while you teach the rest of the class. However, this is not advisable during an Ofsted inspection because all adults should be impacting on pupils' learning. At the end of the year or at the end of a term there will be filing or tidying to do before the school closes and you will want to ensure that you are up to date. Consider whether you can give the pupils an independent task to do to enable you to buy some time to do your own jobs. Clearly you would not do this during an observation or during an inspection but in the real world this can be really helpful. Think about how you might involve the pupils in doing end-of-term jobs. It is faster for thirty people to do something than to try to do everything yourself.

Coping with stress and anxiety

The signs of stress and anxiety can vary from person to person and in teaching, like other professions, stress and anxiety can manifest itself in different ways. Possible signs include:

- tiredness despite sleep
- disrupted sleeping patterns
- over-sleeping
- dizziness
- feelings of being overwhelmed/lack of control
- headaches
- pins and needles
- excessive sweating
- low self-esteem
- racing thoughts
- worry – going over things again and again
- panic attacks
- muscle pain.

This is not an exhaustive list and only your doctor will be able to diagnose whether you are suffering from stress, anxiety or some other medical condition. In teaching, it is not possible to eradicate stress because every new day brings different challenges. An irate parent could send your blood pressure soaring through the roof. Pupils can become distressed or disruptive out of the blue. A colleague could do something to upset you. A no-notice Ofsted inspection is bound to create stress and anxiety, no matter how well prepared you may feel.

The critical thing is that you need to be able to manage the stress so that it does not spiral out of control. There will be times during the academic year that can be considered 'hot-spots'. One example of this is during examination time when pupils' scripts need to be marked. Another example is when pupils' reports need to be written in the summer term. The good thing though is that at least you know when these 'hot-spots' are going to occur, so you can mentally prepare yourself for them. Other situations like those mentioned above cannot be prepared for, but you can manage the way in which you respond to them when they arise.

Establishing clear priorities

Different priorities will emerge at different points during the year. You may find it useful to map out the whole academic year so that you know what jobs need to be completed and by when. Forward planning can alleviate stress because you can allocate time to complete specific tasks. Make sure that you know what the deadlines are for jobs that need to be completed and do not leave things until the last minute. You will tell your pupils this many times but as a teacher it is more difficult for you simply because you have so many jobs to do. Get a diary (paper or electronic format) and set out your priorities clearly. Some tasks will be less urgent and can be done later but others will need to be done more imminently, so you will need to learn how to prioritise.

Conclusion

Teaching is an incredibly demanding but hugely rewarding job. At times you will feel stressed or even anxious and education is placing increasing demands on schools and teachers. This is partly because the government has increased its expectations and school inspections are now even more rigorous. Although it is not possible to take the stress out of teaching, it is possible to manage it well. You will need to be skilled at multi-tasking and you will need to work efficiently in order to complete your roles and responsibilities. If things start to spiral out of control, the first thing you should do is to talk to a trusted colleague. Talking through the challenges can alleviate stress and anxiety and your colleague may be able to offer practical help. If you feel like you are unable to cope with the demands of your job, you should talk to your line manager or leadership team about your workload. If you do not get the necessary help, your teaching union will be there to support you.

What we have learned

- There are many challenges associated with teaching
- A work–life balance is most important
- The need to organise workload, with clear priorities

Advice and ideas (1)

Lists often are a good way of managing your priorities. List the jobs that you need to do each week and tick them off as you complete them. This is very satisfying because you will feel that you are making progress. Unforeseen tasks may arise during the week that need to be prioritised. Simply add these to your list and complete them as soon as possible. Anything that does not get completed one week can then be rolled over to the next week. Writing a list will prevent you from forgetting things.

Advice and ideas (2)

Try to allocate specific evenings during the week when you do not work. Use this time to meet with friends or to be with your family and try not to talk about work. Have one day at the weekend that is not spent on work. You certainly should not need to work all weekend every week, although there may be 'hot-spots' during the year when you do need to spend the whole weekend working.

Try to find time to pursue a hobby or interest that has no link to your job. Some teachers may enjoy visiting the theatre or going to the cinema or even playing golf! Some may prefer to spend their time shopping or visiting places of interest. Try to develop friendships outside of work because if your colleagues become your friends, you will inevitably discuss school when you meet with them. If you have an enriching life outside of school it will make you more interesting to your pupils. No-one will thank you for devoting your life to your job and there is more to life than just teaching!

What do you think . . .

. . . you should do in the holidays? Teachers in maintained schools in England generally have thirteen weeks of the year when they are not required to teach. How much of this time should be allocated to your professional roles and responsibilities?

Problem

How do I manage a marking workload that appears to be endless?

Solution

When planning lessons, consider how you can reduce your marking workload. If you ask your pupils to produce recorded work by the end of every lesson, this could generate well over 100 pieces of work to mark at the end of the day. You do not need written outcomes from every lesson and the pupils do not need to write things down in order to learn. Try to intersperse some practical tasks or discussion tasks into some lessons and consider the range of ways that you might try to get pupils to demonstrate their learning. They could explain their learning through a presentation, a poster, a mind map or even record their ideas on an iPad. They could make a model or make a film. They could demonstrate their learning through a piece of drama. These ideas are likely to motivate and inspire your learners. Don't ask pupils to make notes, but instead give them the notes and spend more of the lesson time carrying out discussions and practical tasks. Consider ways of involving the pupils in marking their own work (self-assessment) or using peer assessment as a way of enabling learners to give feedback to each other (see Chapter 10).

Recommended reading

Day, C. and Kington, A. (2008) Identity, well-being and effectiveness: the emotional contexts of teaching, *Pedagogy, Culture and Society*, 16 (1): 7–23.

CHAPTER 15

Research and being reflective

What this chapter covers

- An introduction to models of reflective practice

- How to critically reflect on your practice using different tools

- An introduction to professional inquiry as a basis for professional development

Links to Teachers' Standards

Standards Part One
Standards Group 8: Fulfilment of wider professional responsibilities

Introduction

The Teachers' Standards (DfE, 2013) are underpinned by an expectation that teachers will engage in professional development and a requirement to critically reflect on their own practice. The preamble to the Standards outlines that teachers should be 'self-critical' and, in the Standards, teachers must 'reflect systematically on the effectiveness of lessons and approaches to teaching', 'take responsibility for improving teaching through appropriate professional development', 'adapt teaching to respond to the strengths and needs of all pupils', and 'demonstrate a critical understanding of developments in the subject and curriculum areas, and promote the value of scholarship'.

As a teacher you are accountable for pupils' attainment, progress and outcomes, and through reflection must ensure that the learning activities you plan enable pupils to progress to the next stage of their learning. It also helps you to develop alternative strategies to help pupils to learn when these are needed. Reflection is deeply connected to formative assessment in the classroom. Your focus on the pupils' reactions during explanations, progress with activities, answers to questions during interventions, the questions that they ask and their responses during plenary activities inform your thinking. Reflection helps you to make connections between theories and practice and gradually develops your own knowledge, understanding and pedagogy.

Models of critical reflection

Donald Schön (1983) identified two types of reflection. The first, *reflection-in-action* refers to the quick decisions we make in response to stimuli during the course of a lesson. These decisions are informed by our prior experience, practice-based knowledge and internalised theoretical knowledge, which Schön called 'knowledge in action'. Reflection-in-action is the sort of reflection that happens when teachers 'think on their feet', drawing on a repertoire of previously successful strategies or coming up with a new solution.

For example, imagine a situation when pupils have been asked to move into groups to complete a collaborative activity. One pupil refuses to go into the allocated group and the teacher first tries to persuade him to do so, to no avail. The teacher very quickly has to make decisions such as how the pupil can complete the task independently or whether they should use the assertive discipline procedure to coax the pupil into joining the group. This decision draws on knowledge of previous interactions with the pupil, previous experience of managing group work and knowledge of how the task might be completed a different way. Reflection-in-action involves very quickly considering the implications of each choice during the course of the interaction.

In contrast, *reflection-on-action* occurs after the event and is a much more systematic type of reflection. It involves a deeper consideration of what led to the situation, what influenced the teacher's actions and the actions of the pupil, an evaluation of the success of the action and consideration of possible alternative courses of action. For trainee teachers, this reflection-on-action may happen with the support of their mentor and it may involve some form of knowledge development, such as learning about alternative ways of grouping pupils or observing a more experienced teacher with a particular focus on transitions between activities.

The process of reflection during training can be closely aligned with Kolb's (1984) experiential learning cycle. In this cyclical model of learning, the *concrete experience*, in our case classroom practice, is central to the learning process. Kolb's model is based on the premise that it is impossible to learn effectively from reading or study alone, that active experience is key. The next stage is called *reflective observation*. In this stage, the learner steps back from 'doing' and reviews the experience. For us, this stage might involve an observation of our practice, a discussion with our mentor, and a focus on the outcomes the pupils have produced during the lesson. The third stage is *abstract conceptualisation*, which involves a deeper analysis, interpretation and evaluation of practice and may include references to theory to support the framing and explanation of events. The final stage is *active experimentation*, when the learner plans the actions that should be taken as a result of the reflection, what they will do differently as a result. This feeds into the next cycle of concrete experience, reflective observation, and so on.

Brookfield (1995) suggests that effective reflection involves 'viewing' the experience from different perspectives. Brookfield proposes four 'lenses' or perspectives to aid teachers' reflection: autobiographical, student, peer and theoretical. Focus on the *autobiographical* perspective involves reflecting on the classroom experience in light of a personal philosophy of teaching in order to become more aware of the values and assumptions that underpin teaching. The *student* lens enables the teacher to understand the pupils' experiences and to evaluate the teaching from their point of view. The *peer* lens for trainee teachers is about reflecting on their teaching in light of the advice and feedback of their mentor. The final lens involves reflection in light of *theoretical* perspectives and references to literature.

Making use of research

These are just two examples of research-based adaptations to practice. There is a huge body of research into education, so it would be foolish of you not to use it to support your development. There are, however, a few caveats. First, check the date of the research: if it rather dated, there are likely to be more recent papers and publications building on it or critiquing it. If it is old, but seminal – for example, Bloom's (1956) taxonomy or Gardner's (1983) multiple intelligences – this means that you can quote the original, but also means that this was the 'seed' for many other developments, so there will be more recent writings. Second, check on its geographical location – a lot is American or Antipodean, so may not apply to your local systems. Third, check its authenticity – Wikipedia and random blogs and websites carry little by way of cachet. As a teacher you will often be told that there is no point in re-inventing the wheel so, before you do so, check on the research. Improvements in teaching are driven by research – you can both use it and contribute to it.

Tools for reflection

You can look on lesson evaluations as 'mini' pieces of research – collecting and evaluating evidence and practice. Lesson evaluations are an expectation of most teacher education programmes, and it is easy for these to become tedious and repetitive if you view them as just another paper exercise on a long list of paper exercises needed to complete your course. Lesson evaluations are the formal way in which you demonstrate critical reflection on your teaching and learning. To see the importance of these, it might help you to focus on the two principal functions of evaluations during your training year. The first is to help you to plan subsequent learning experiences for the pupils in your care;

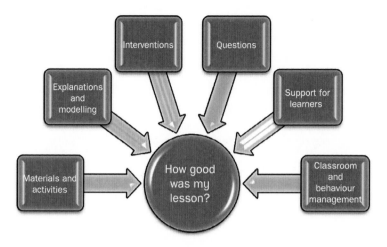

there should be an obvious connection between your lesson plan and the previous lesson evaluation. The second is to help you to develop your teaching skills and classroom practice. It is important therefore for lesson evaluations to focus on particular aspects of practice in order to help you to make systematic progress.

Areas that might be important include:

- **The materials and activities designed for pupils.** Were they engaging? Did they enable pupils to find out for themselves? How did they develop pupils' understanding? Did all pupils engage with them?
- **Your explanations and modelling.** Did they help pupils to grasp the concept? What questions did they ask? Could they engage in the task quickly afterwards? In what ways did you need to reinforce the exposition?
- **Your interventions.** What did they tell you about the pupils' understanding? What impact did they have on the outcomes? Did all pupils benefit?
- **Your questions.** How did these engage pupils? Which pupils volunteered answers? Why? How did you stretch and challenge learners?
- **Supporting learners.** What was effective in supporting different learners in the lesson? Who surprised you? How can you help them further next lesson?
- **Classroom and behaviour management.** What were the stressful parts of the lesson for you? Who did you further develop a relationship with today? How? How could you have handled a situation better? Why? Was the organisation of the classroom and resources effective?

These questions are by no means exhaustive, nor are they meant to be prescriptive. Although you could answer some of them with a yes/no response, they are intended to stimulate critical thinking about the decisions you made both before (your planning) and during the lesson.

Reflections on classroom experiences

In addition to lesson evaluations, other stimuli can help you to reflect on your classroom experiences and to develop your practice:

- **Learning journal.** A learning journal is a personal document. It contains experiences, thoughts, feelings, descriptions, reflections on events over a period of time. The most important part of the process of keeping a journal is to build in time to reflect on and analyse what you have written to help you 'take stock' of your learning, to make comparisons with theoretical perspectives and to identify further areas for development.

- **Critical incident analysis.** A critical incident is any event or an interaction that made you stop and think differently about an aspect of your practice. It is not necessarily a dramatic event, it could be something that a pupil or a mentor has said, or a piece of work that a pupil has produced, or a reaction to an aspect of your teaching that you were not expecting. To reflect on a critical incident, you need to write an analytical account in which you note your feelings, consider the appropriateness of your actions, identify the assumptions you made, consider the incident from the other person's perspective, ask how else you could interpret the situation and what other actions could be taken, summarise your learning from the incident and articulate what you will do differently in the future.

- **Critical friendship.** A critical friend can support you to develop your practice over a period of time through collaborative reflection. They can provide practical support by giving you the confidence to try different things and by encouraging you to take risks. Their role is to ask questions that challenge your thinking and assumptions. They can help you to consider alternatives and broker access to other people's practice. They can aid inquiry by collecting evidence through observation or discussion with pupils. During your training year, your mentor will provide critical friendship, but another trainee or later a colleague could take on this role.

- **SWOT analysis.** Such an analysis can help you to focus on a particular aspect of your practice and identify an action plan for further development. It focuses on identifying your Strengths and Weaknesses or areas for further development, the Opportunities for developing your practice and the Threats – the possible barriers to success. For our purposes, you might think of the strengths as the things you are doing well in the classroom and the confidence this gives you in tackling the things that need further development. Considering opportunities is about identifying the resources you can employ to help you develop your practice and planning how you will do things differently as a result. Considering the threats encourages you to think of the possible problems you might encounter and what you can to mitigate these.

- **Video.** Videotaping a part of the lesson can be one of the most powerful ways to help you to engage in reflective practice. This really helps you to see yourself as the pupils see you. Once you have got over the shock of seeing yourself on screen, careful analysis of the pupils' reactions to your teaching helps you to identify what is effective and how you can improve. It can help you to focus on individual pupils' progress and engagement and often identifies areas for consideration you might have missed in the course of normal evaluation.

Effective critical reflection might thus be summarised as a systematic unpicking of the issues and moving from description to thinking about why events happened as they did. It involves questioning our own assumptions. For example, it is easy to assume that a behavioural issue is a problem connected to the child, but what other explanation might there be? We should view issues from different perspectives and move from focusing on the teaching to a focus on the pupils' learning. Critical reflection also needs to be supported by a range of evidence; we need to ask ourselves how we know our assertions are correct.

Developing critical reflection into more formal methods of teacher inquiry is a natural evolution. Teaching is an evidence-based profession where improvements come about through theories, methods and interventions being trialled in the classroom. Engaging in classroom inquiry can be a powerful vehicle for your further professional development and career advancement.

Action research

Action research is a form of practitioner research derived from reflective practice and experiential learning. It differs from the everyday critical reflection of teachers in that it involves the systematic collection of evidence. It is characterised by inquiry that is focused on problems identified by teachers themselves.

Action research is simply a form of self-reflective enquiry undertaken by participants in social situations in order to improve the rationality and justice of their own practices, their understanding of these practices, and the situations in which the practices are carried out.

(Carr and Kemmis, 1986: 162)

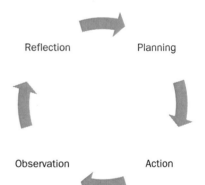

Reflection   Planning

Observation   Action

In action research, the inquiry is related to improving practice and therefore the data collected is focused on identifying the impact of an intervention. Action research is a cyclical or spiral process of planning, action, observation and reflection:

- The *planning stage* of the process involves identifying the issue, fact finding and gathering evidence of the extent of the problem to use as a basis for evaluating impact. Fact finding includes exploring what other research tells us about the issue under investigation. This informs our understanding and helps us to identify and develop the actions or intervention that would be appropriate to trial in the classroom. The planning stage also involves considering the methods that will be used to gather data to measure impact.

- The *action stage* is the implementation of the intervention. The nature of the intervention depends on the inquiry, but usually includes a change in practice and a focus on a different way of doing things.
- The *observation stage* is the monitoring of the intervention and the collection of data to inform your reflection.
- *Reflection* involves analysing the data to evaluate the impact of the intervention and make recommendations for future practice. At this point, you may want to disseminate your findings to colleagues. In this stage, you also outline the next steps, the changes in practice that are important to maintain and perhaps areas that would benefit from further development and investigation, leading to another cycle of planning, action, observation and reflection.

Conclusion

Whether part of a more formal practitioner inquiry or not, critical reflection lends itself to the use of data that is collected as a normal part of lessons as well as the more traditional forms of data collections such as interviews, questionnaires, focus groups and case studies. Woodhouse (2012) suggests that samples of pupils' work, assessment information and records such as behaviour logs are useful forms of data to analyse. Video recording the lesson or audio recording pupils' discourse as they work on tasks collaboratively could also provide rich data to inform your inquiry. Using a colleague such as a support assistant or a mentor to collect data during the lesson such as keeping a tally of how many open or closed questions you ask (see Chapter 8), or observing specific pupils' responses to tasks and interventions (see Chapter 2) can be really powerful in enabling deep evaluation of your work.

Evidence such as this is context specific, but the aim of practitioner research is to improve your own practice, not necessarily to find solutions that are more widely generalisable. The benefits of systematic reflection for teaching and learning in your classroom are clear. Thorough reflection and evaluation will help you to feel more empowered to try different strategies to support your development.

What we have learned

- Critical reflection is an essential process in planning learning opportunities for pupils that are appropriate to aid their progression
- Critical reflection enables us to systematically improve our own practice and is essential for our professional development

Advice and ideas (1)

Being critical also applies when reading. For non-critical readers, sources provide 'facts' and the purpose of reading is to absorb these facts to help develop an understanding of the topic under investigation. Critical readers recognise that a source contains only *one* version of the facts and that in order to gain a full understanding, the text must be interrogated, the reasoning and evidence provided must be evaluated, and the author's values and perspectives taken into account (Price, 2012: 19).

Advice and ideas (2)

Teacher inquiry can be presented formally as a presentation or a poster for dissemination, or written up as a paper as part of a Master's level study programme. Reflecting on the following questions will enable you to analyse your study more critically:

Consideration of context and values

- To what extent are the findings unique to a particular context?
- What are the underlying values that shape our practice?

Consideration of literature

- What are the key debates?
- What are the key criticisms and limitations?
- To what extent are they useful?

Critically reflecting on own practice

- How is your practice underpinned by theoretical frameworks?
- What is the impact on students' learning?
- What evidence supports your analysis?

Reflecting on learning

- How has the study enhanced your professional development?

What do you think . . .

Your teacher identity is built from your ideas, aspirations and philosophical understanding of the purposes of your role. In defining a concept of yourself as a teacher, you look at ideas we embrace and those we discard. Think of two teachers whom you most admire. What aspects of their teaching do you find compelling? How do they engage pupils in their learning? In five key words, how would you describe their teaching? How is your teaching similar to theirs? How is it different?

Problem

You are overwhelmed by the areas you could write about in your evaluation.

Solution

Discipline yourself to focus on one or two areas of your practice that have been identified in your conversations with your mentor as key areas for development at the current time. Try a different tool to support your reflections from the examples given.

Recommended reading

Brookfield, S. (1995) *Becoming a Critically Reflective Teacher*. San Francisco, CA: Jossey-Bass.

Carr, W. and Kemmis, S. (1986) *Becoming Critical: Education, Knowledge and Action Research*. Lewes: Falmer Press.

Department for Education (DfE) (2013) *The Teachers' Standards*. Available at: https://www.gov.uk/government/uploads/system/uploads/attachment_data/file/208682/Teachers__Standards_2013.pdf.

Kolb, D.A. (1984) *Experiential Learning: Experience as the Source of Learning and Development*. Englewood Cliffs, NJ: Prentice-Hall.

Price, J. (2012) Reading for teacher inquiry, in N. Mitchell and J. Pearson (eds) *Inquiring in the Classroom*. London: Continuum.

Schön, D. (1983) *The Reflective Practitioner*. San Francisco, CA: Jossey-Bass.

Woodhouse, F. (2012) Research in teaching: how to harness everyday teaching activities as teacher enquiry methods, in N. Mitchell and J. Pearson (eds) *Inquiring in the Classroom*. London: Continuum.

Zwozdiak-Myers, P. (2012) *The Teacher's Reflective Practice Handbook: Becoming an Extended Professional through Capturing Evidence-informed Practice*. London: Routledge.

16

The application and interview process

Introduction

As a trainee teacher you will have worked alongside qualified teachers and school leadership teams who will have been accountable for the pupils in their care. As a newly qualified teacher you will now be accountable for the safety, wellbeing, progress and attainment of your pupils. You should not take this responsibility lightly. As a teacher you will be placed in the privileged position of being able to make a positive difference to pupils' education and their lives. Not only are you accountable to your pupils, but also to school leadership teams, the local authority (in state-maintained schools), parents and carers, governors and the government. You will ultimately be held to account if you and your pupils do not perform and you may have to face penalties if your capability is called into question. Teaching is an increasingly challenging profession. It is also extremely rewarding. You will find that no two days are alike. Each day brings new challenges and often there are no easy solutions. During your initial teacher training you will have been 'cushioned' by your mentors from dealing with challenging situations with pupils, parents and other colleagues. Now you will have to face those challenges head on, but with the support of your colleagues.

Looking for teaching posts

It is rare that a teaching post will come looking for you, although this can happen. Some trainees secure posts in their placement schools on the strength of their performance. Some training routes now almost guarantee a job, at least for a year. Most of you, however, will need to go through the process of searching for jobs, writing applications and attending interviews. Don't expect to secure the first post for which you apply. If you are not shortlisted, request feedback from the school so that you can strengthen subsequent applications.

Most teaching posts are advertised from January through to July, although a few may be advertised earlier or later than this. There is usually an increase after 31 May, which is when serving teachers are required to submit their resignations to governing bodies. Many teaching posts are advertised in the *Times Educational Supplement*, which is published every Friday. You can also access these same posts on line by visiting www.tes.co.uk.

Advertising in the *Times Educational Supplement* can be expensive and consequently schools may choose to advertise their posts on the local authority website and/or their own website. This is free for schools. Many schools will advertise vacancies in more than one way. Vacancies are also advertised through supply teacher agency websites and increasingly circulated via social networking sites.

Preparing an application

Before making an application, think carefully about the type of school in which you want to work. You may wish to ask yourself the following questions. Do I want to work . . .

- in a rural, suburban or inner-city school?
- within an affluent area or one of social deprivation?
- in a large or small school?
- on a team with relatively young or more experienced staff?
- in a school with pupils who have English as an additional language?
- in a school with a high or low proportion of pupils with special educational needs?
- in a school with resourced provision for pupils with special educational needs?
- in a special school?
- in a local authority school, Academy or free school?

- in a faith school?
- in a school judged at a particular level by Ofsted? (Newly qualified teachers cannot work in schools that have been placed in Special Measures.)

These questions (and others like them) will help you to think about the type of school in which you want to work. You may have to be more flexible if you find that by July you have not secured a post, but there is nothing wrong with initially trying to find a job in the kind of school in which you would choose to work.

Finding information

Once you have spotted an advertisement and you are interested in a post, take some time to look at the school website to glean more information. Many schools now upload the school policies, self-evaluation and improvement plans on their websites, so read these carefully. Visit the Ofsted website (www.ofsted.gov.uk) to access the latest inspection report.

Read the advertisement carefully. If it refers to 'inclusion', this could indicate that there is a high proportion of pupils with special educational needs. If it makes reference to 'lively pupils', this could indicate that there are pupils with challenging behaviour. You might not mind working with pupils like this but you would mind if managing behaviour was not one of your strong points. Read between the lines and look for the clues.

Visiting the school

Many advertisements state that visits to the school are 'warmly welcomed'. In reality, many head teachers will expect you to have visited the school before you apply for a post or at least before you attend an interview. Telephone the school and make an appointment; where possible, try to arrange your visit during the working day so that you can see the school in operation. You may find that a specific time has been allocated for visits, and if this is the case you will have to be flexible and fit in with the school.

Think carefully about your dress code during the visit. Dress smartly. It is not part of the interview but people will formulate initial impressions of you. Use the visit as an opportunity to find out if this is the kind of school in which you want to work. Be friendly and polite and ask questions about the school. Do not ask questions that you should already know the answers to from your initial research about the school. You might want to ask about pupils' progress and attainment because access to the most up-to-date information is always helpful. However, do not ask too many questions.

At the end of the visit, thank the person showing you round and always be polite and courteous to all staff, including administrative staff. Often, they will be asked for their opinions about you after you leave. As you walk away from the school, maintain your professionalism, at least until you are well out of the way. Lighting up a cigarette in the playground or just outside the premises is really not a good idea! After the visit you should be sure about whether you want to apply for the post.

Writing an application

Application packs will contain details of the post (a job specification) and of the ideal candidate (a person specification). The person specification lists the essential and desirable characteristics that the applicant should be able to demonstrate. You will have to show how you meet the essential criteria for the post and what elements of the desirable characteristics you can evidence. Often you can download the application form and complete it electronically; sometimes you have to complete it by hand. Sometimes you may need to telephone to receive it. Complete all sections of the application form carefully and as stipulated in any guidance that you receive.

Writing personal statements

You will usually be asked for a personal statement to support your application. Do not send a curriculum vitae unless this is specifically requested. The biggest mistake that applicants make when writing personal statements is that they are too general and do not relate specifically to the school. The opening paragraph should begin by stating why you want to work in **this** school. Don't write an academic essay – head teachers will not be impressed by your ability to cite academic theorists, literature or research. You are now applying to work in the real world! Use the personal statement to convey your own beliefs, values and principles about teaching. The following structure might help:

- Head your statement appropriately, e.g. 'Teacher of Business and Economics. Post Reference 1234. Personal Statement'.
- Address the head teacher as he or she appears on the school's notepaper, e.g. Dear Dr. Smith, Dear Mrs. Kauser.
- Include a paragraph to say why you want to work in **this** school.
- Talk about the different experiences and your performance in placement schools plus any previous experience you have had in schools.
- Discuss any training that you have attended and its impact.
- Give examples of good and outstanding lessons you have taught and briefly describe them.
- Talk about how you have used assessment in your teaching.
- Talk about the strategies you have used to manage pupils' behaviour.
- Talk about how and why you have differentiated your lessons.
- Talk about your own beliefs in terms of how you think pupils learn and the characteristics of an effective learning environment.
- Discuss how you have worked as part of teams in school, including how you have worked with support staff and other colleagues, parents and the wider community.
- Explain how you have contributed to the wider life of the schools in which you have worked.

- Include something that will make you stand out from the crowd such as a special skill that you have.

There are three critical points that you need to bear in mind when you complete your personal statement:

1. Whenever you mention something, validate it with a practical example from your practice. For example, if you want to make a point that you believe that teachers should be creative or that learning should be active, give examples of what you have done to demonstrate this.
2. Address all the 'essential' criteria on the person specification. This is important, as these are used for shortlisting. The person specification will usually indicate which criteria are being assessed in the application form and which in the interview.
3. Make as much of the personal statement as possible relate to **this** school. You have visited the school and have gained a great deal of knowledge. Communicate why you want to work **here** and when you talk about assessment, behaviour management and learning environments don't just mention what you have done, but refer to what **this** school does and why this excites you.

The interview

If you complete the application form carefully and correctly and you meet all the criteria, you should be shortlisted. The school will ring you or write to you to invite you to an interview and provide you with an outline of what the interview will entail. It is now standard practice for candidates to be asked to demonstrate their teaching skills to either a class or group of pupils. The timings of this exercise will vary from school to school from anything as short as ten minutes to an hour. Secondary school applicants will usually be asked to teach their specialist subject, usually with a clear focus given for the lesson. Primary school applicants could be asked to teach any subject to any year group and may or may not be given a specific focus.

Preparing the lesson

You might be provided with information to help you prepare for the lesson, including the pupils' prior learning, details of pupils' abilities and whether you will have access to a teaching assistant or ICT. If you are not provided with this information you can telephone the school to ask. The school may refuse to supply the information but they will possibly make a note that you have requested this and this will go in your favour.

Produce a lesson plan and make sure that you identify clear learning objectives and success criteria for the pupils. Don't plan too much for the allocated time but it is imperative that the pupils are seen to make progress. Keep resources to a minimum so that you are not overloaded, and if you plan to use ICT, have a back-up plan in case it fails to work on the day.

Teaching the lesson

Wake up in good time and have breakfast. You will need it for energy. Take some bottled water with you to keep you hydrated. Plan your journey to the school so that you arrive in good time. Your pre-visit may have taken place during the day but if you are required to arrive first thing in the morning, the travelling time may well be different. Dress smartly by wearing a suit and smart shoes. Avoid low-cut tops and short skirts that may be too revealing. You might not normally dress in this way but you are attending an interview and there are protocols. You might also want to think about whether your piercings and tattoos – however much they are a part of 'you' – are appropriate.

Stay calm on the day. The lesson will be observed by the head teacher and possibly other members of the leadership team and governors. When the lesson starts, remember to introduce yourself to the pupils and don't forget to tell them what they are learning.

Individual interview

Once the lesson is over, there will be an individual interview. You might have to spend a substantial part of the day waiting for your interview and other staff who work in the school may come to talk to you. Remember that you are being assessed all the time. You will be interviewed by a panel of people, usually the head teacher, deputy head teacher, other teachers and governors. Remember that some of the governors are also parents who may not understand the professional language of teaching, so avoid the use of acronyms or jargon and pitch your responses to the audience instead of using complex terminology, which may act as a barrier.

It is common practice for the panel to introduce themselves to you. You will feel nervous but try to smile at them. They may well be just as nervous as you! You will then be asked a series of questions. It is important to answer the question that has been asked rather than what you think has been asked. If you need a question to be repeated or you need some thinking time, do not be afraid to ask. Sometimes you can predict the questions that you will be asked by reading the person specification, although some of the questions will be a surprise to you. If you are given the opportunity to reflect on the lesson that you taught, remember to talk about what worked well but also acknowledge the improvements you would make. When you offer your responses to each question, try to give as much detail as possible but do not waffle and do not repeat yourself. Try to bring into your answers examples of what you have done during your placements and during your previous experiences in school to address these aspects of professional practice. Possible questions that you could be asked during the interview include:

- Tell us what you can bring to this school
- Tell us why you are keen to work in this school
- Tell us how you would raise standards of achievement and attainment for all pupils
- If I walked into your classroom, what would it look like?

- In this school there are several pupils with SEN and other vulnerable learners. What strategies could you use to improve outcomes for these pupils?
- What strategies would you use to manage pupils' behaviour?
- How do you use assessment to improve outcomes for pupils?
- Tell us about your best and worst lesson.
- How do you see your career developing?
- What attracted you to this post?
- How would you work in partnership with parents?
- How would you work in partnership with pupils?
- How do you see yourself fitting into our team?
- How would you deal with a disclosure of abuse or suspected abuse?
- How would you cater for different learning needs?
- How can you contribute to the religious values/general ethos of this school?

At the end of the interview you may be asked if you have any questions yourself. This is not a test and if you do not need to ask a question, simply acknowledge this by stating that all of your questions have been answered. Before you leave the room thank the panel for their time.

You may also be interviewed by the student council or other pupils. Be friendly and polite with the pupils, tell them how you will make their learning fun and ask them what they are looking for in a teacher and what sort of things they would like you to do. This turns the interview on its head!

The decision who to appoint is almost always made on the day. It used to be common practice for all interviewees to sit together and wait for the decision, often into the twilight! Nowadays, it is more usual to be released after the formal interview and contacted by telephone.

Supply teaching

Supply teaching should not be classed as second-rate teaching. Indeed, many teachers choose supply work because they may need more flexibility with their working lives. This could be as a result of family circumstances. There are many supply agencies and you can shop around to get the best deal. You might be able to secure long-term, short-term or day-to-day contracts and will be able to specify the types of schools in which you want to work, their locations and your preferred age ranges. You will be interviewed by the agency and this is typically more relaxed than a traditional teaching interview. The agency will agree with you a rate of pay and they will take a cut from this for managing your work.

Supply teaching will give you experience working in a range of schools and it will get you known! Many supply teachers secure permanent posts in the schools where they have worked on account of their reputation. Head teachers may recommend you to other heads. You can complete your induction on supply if you can secure a term's contract and the school can provide the necessary support. You cannot complete your induction on daily supply in different schools. The drawback to supply is that there may be periods of time when you are not able to secure work. September is typically a quiet time for supply teachers.

Conclusion

There is no guarantee that you will be successful, especially on the first interview. Ask your training provider or a head teacher to conduct a mock interview with you, also to comment on your personal statement. On many routes, this will happen as standard. To secure your first teaching post you will need to jump through various hoops. Don't make promises during the interview that you cannot keep. There is little point in declaring that you have a passion for sport if you are not prepared to run an after-school sports club. Never be unprofessional during interviews by referring to other schools or teachers in ways that are demeaning or belittling. Stay calm, stay professional and remember to smile! You will get there eventually!

What we have learned

- How to write a personal statement
- How to succeed in an interview
- The advantages and disadvantages of supply teaching

Advice and ideas (1)

Have a friend check your personal statement and application form. You may miss errors yourself. Also beware the American spellchecker and try to avoid jargon. Spelling, grammar and punctuation errors are inexcusable and if they are evident on your application, you can expect it to be consigned to the bin! Be particularly careful with commas, semi-colons and apostrophes, as these are frequently used incorrectly. If you cannot be bothered with your written English or to complete the form correctly, why should the school assume that you will take care with the job should you be offered it?

Advice and ideas (2)

If you are unlucky and you do not secure the job, you will usually be offered feedback. Take advantage of this and use it to improve your performance in subsequent interviews. Do not be disheartened. Pick yourself up, dust yourself down and try again. The more interviews you do, the more your confidence will grow.

What do you think . . .

Can your personal statement be too school specific? Personal statements often do not make enough reference to the school itself, apart from perhaps an opening paragraph on why you want to work in the school. Refer to the school in every section of the application. Avoid creating the impression that you have run off a personal statement that you used for a different school.

Problem

You are invited to two interviews on two consecutive days but the second interview is the job that you really want. You are offered the first post. You face the dilemma of whether to accept the post, whether to decline it or whether to ask for additional time to help you decide what to do.

Solution

At the end of the interview you should have been asked to confirm your interest in taking up the post should the job be offered to you. This would be the time to withdraw if you are uncertain. You can also withdraw from the process at any point up to the point of being offered the job. If you are offered the job, you should accept it at this point. You may not secure the post on the second interview and at the point of being offered a job the governors will assume that you want it. It is unreasonable to ask governors to wait before you make a decision. This could damage your reputation and it communicates a clear message that the first interview was for your second-choice post.

Recommended reading

Ainsworth, P.K. (2012) *Get that Teaching Job.* London: Continuum.

Robinson, C., Bingle, B. and Howard, C. (2013) Employability, in *Primary School Placements: A Critical Guide to Outstanding Teaching*, Northwich: Critical Publishing.

Index